REFLECTIONS
on the
PAST
and the
FUTURE

TO DEE DEE

REFLECTIONS
on the
PAST
and the
FUTURE

CARL FREEMAN REYNOLDS

Copyright © 2013 by Carl Freeman Reynolds.

cover photo by Carl F. Reynolds

ISBN:	Softcover	978-1-4931-1721-5
	Ebook	978-1-4931-1722-2

All rights reserved. No part of this book may be reproduced or transmitted in any form or by any means, electronic or mechanical, including photocopying, recording, or by any information storage and retrieval system, without permission in writing from the copyright owner.

This book was printed in the United States of America.

Rev. date: 10/17/2013

To order additional copies of this book, contact:
Xlibris LLC
1-888-795-4274
www.Xlibris.com
Orders@Xlibris.com
142283

Contents

Prelude 9
Common Union 13
In The Beginning 17
In Spirit and In Truth 22
One God . . . Many Names 27
The Art Of Living 32
For the Love of God 37
Goin Home 42
You Gotta Serve Somebody 44
He/She/His/Hers/Him/Her: God 49
Walking In the Dark 55
Giving Thanks—Letting Go—Letting God 58
What Time Is It? 62
What Are We Waiting For? Hope! 66
Peace 71
Love 76
Christ Is Come! 81
". . . from the East . . ." 83
Baptized With Spirit and Fire 90
The Lord's Prayer 95
Transfigured or Only A Dream 100
To The End Of The Age 104
Gone Fishin' 110
Sing a New Song 115
". . . and they all understood each other . . ." 119
In Memory of Peace 124
That All May Be One 129
God is Still Speaking . . . Are We Still Listening? 133
In the Eye of the Beholder 138
Sacrament 143
Who We Can Be 148

Prophecy	152
King of the Jews	157
The Door Is Open	162
Glory and Honor	167
Little Children	172
A Big Heart Open to God	177
On Being Made Whole	182

Dedication

The words of this book are dedicated to my wife, Debra, my three daughters: Marinda, Julia and Katrina, my two granddaughters, Amelia and Meadow and the wonderful folks who make up the Second Congregational Church of Stafford Springs at West Stafford, CT for whom these words were written.

Prelude

It's been a quiet few months up here in my newly adopted hometown of Stafford Springs, West Stafford to be specific, up here on the northern edge of Connecticut, just south of the tornado ravaged state of Massachusetts. It's especially quiet this time of year: the speedway is closed and it's too cold to ride motorcycles, but the supersized pickup trucks and overloaded semis pretty well make up for their absence. It's especially quiet mostly because we've got all our storm windows and storm doors battened down to keep the cold out and the woodstove warm in.

Stafford Springs has been able to maintain its insulation against mc-mansion overkill and shopping mall sprawl that has overwhelmed most towns to the west of here, but it has a nice collection of restaurants, a hardware store, a few antique if not junk shops, a Big Y and a small Stafford Food Market and a collection of other little shops and stores. It also hosts ten Churches of various denominations. You come over Somers Mountain on route 140 or 190 and it's like coming down into a somewhat different world; like an older Connecticut. It reminds of me a lot of some of my former adopted home towns in Vermont, New Hampshire and Maine, even Farmington, Ct where I grew up before I-84, the Stacks, the West Farms Mall, and seemingly countless housing developments buried all the open spaces I once wandered as a kid. Stafford Springs is a nice place to be.

I must have driven by this Church a thousand times over the years, and never thought I'd be up here doing this. I was ordained in 1977 and spent the first three years of ordination as the Director of Outdoor Ministries for the Vermont Conference, UCC. I then served a three Church Parish in central Vermont; the largest had 32 members, the medium one had 25 members and the small one had 21 members, and on every given Sunday every member of that little congregation was accounted for before we could begin worship; three services every Sunday, three collections of meetings every month. That too was a nice place to be. Then I did a short stint in Outdoor Ministry in the New York Conference, UCC. That was not a nice place to be. Next I ended up in the Canterbury (NH) United Community Church; UCC and American Baptist. That was a great place to be; the only Church in town; members of every denomination imaginable. I was a Captain in the volunteer fire department; a real homey home town. We probably would have stayed there except we wanted our daughters to have a more diverse and inclusive environment to grow up in, so we ended up in East Windsor, CT for the next eight or so years; another nice adopted home town. I spent the next twelve or so years out of the Church; though I spent 9 ½ years installed as the Senior Construction Supervisor for Hartford Area Habitat for Humanity where I taught people how to build houses instead of Churches for people who had never had a home. I spent a year and a half on the dole, got my profile back in circulation and one day I opened up the UCC Employment Opportunity listings and there was the Second Congregational Church of Stafford at West Stafford. Two weeks later I had an interview and three weeks after that I did a candidating service and got called. What really sold me was that the Search Committee made a most remarkable statement: "We know we are dwindling; we know we have to grow in order to survive; we know we have to be willing to change in order to grow." You have no idea how much blood, sweat and tears; how much time and energy I had invested in other Churches trying to convince them that that was true, with very little success, and here that truth was handed to me on a silver platter. Like every other organic, living entity on earth, the Church must evolve; it must grow in order to survive; not change just for the sake of change but evolution growing out of our firm foundations: enhanced by innovation, creativity, new ways of expressing and living out our faith.

 I know the intent of this missal is to tell you something about how I envision my ministry, not necessarily to try to emulate one of my heroes, Garrison Kieller, and I want to do that as simply and concisely as possible. During my last year at Bangor Theological Seminary I took a tutorial with my Theology professor, the Rev. Dr. Leslie Zeigler, as a summation; a review of the primary theological issues I had learned in seminary. At our last meeting I asked Dr. Zeigler a question: "You have taught me well about many different theologies and theologians . . . which one is right?" She smiled (which she rarely did) and said, "None of them. Theology is a work in process and now you are part of that process." That pretty much sums up my ordained life. When I was first out of seminary my sermons were actually academic presentations of theological concerns, just like all my seminary papers had been. But I had questions festering down inside me, like who says my version of Christianity is right and every other version is wrong; who says Christianity is right and every other religion is wrong? How can there be such major differences between religions, to the point of war, if there is but one God? I didn't really have a place in which I could voice those questions, outside of a close circle of friends, until I was introduced to Matthew Fox and Creation Spirituality some years ago now, which blew open the doors to my questions, allowed me to ask and explore them, and my life hasn't been the same since.

Which religion is right? None of them; religion is a work in progress and we are (or should be) each and all a part of that process. There are more and more open dialogs emerging not just among various Christian denominations, but among various religions. Like the parable about the group of blind people each touching a different part of an elephant and each coming to the conclusion that they know what an elephant really is and everybody else is wrong, people are starting to realize that maybe, just maybe, people of all religions are touching a different part of God (by many names in many images), and if we all got our hearts and minds together, and our doctrines and dogmas out of the way, we just might find that together we could piece together a much bigger and more inclusive image of who and what God is, how God relates to us and how we can and should relate to God and each other.

Now don't in any way get me wrong here: I am in no way insinuating in any way that Christianity is somehow wrong, though I freely admit I have big problems with many of the non-biblically based doctrines and dogmas that the Church created and inserted into the original biblically based Christianity. What I am saying is that as Christians we can and should open ourselves up to other religions not necessarily seeing them as adversaries (though others may see us as adversaries), but to see what God looks like from their points of view. If we do that; if we really believe there is one God known by many names and envisioned in many images, we just might find ourselves somewhat enlightened to a wondrous truth of the power of the presence of God, and open to a more vibrant and creative faith; we just might get a more full and inclusive image of the elephant.

That's the news from West Stafford where everyone is strong, everyone is good looking and everyone is above average. This program was written by cerebellum and the Holy Spirit.

Common Union

We define who we are, at least in part, by what groups of people we are a part of. I am a son, a brother, a father, a grandfather, etc.: I am part of a family. That is one way I define who I am. I am also a photographer, a wood-turner, a carpenter, a cabinet maker and occasionally a poet: I am an artist; a part of the artistic community. That's another way I define who I am. I am also a pastor, a preacher, a teacher, and a spiritual and theological explorer; I am part of the religious community; specifically the Christian community. Stir all of those aspects together with a good measure of various idiosyncrasies, and you've me: Carl; Carl Freeman Reynolds; The Rev. Carl Freeman Reynolds; the family man, the artist, the spiritual and theological explorer. I am an individual to be sure, made up of all those parts. I am a Freeman, as my middle name attests to, and of which I am very humbly proud. But even my most powerful and intentional expressions of my individuality are formed and defined by the people and the groups of people I identify with; the people and groups of people I am a part of and who are a part of me.

Sorry, Simon and Garfunkel, no one is a rock and no one is an island unto themselves. Even if we are reclusive and seclusive and exist/live alone, we got that way by our relationships we were and/or are a part of. If nothing else, we English speakers (or speakers of any language) all share a common language, which defines how we think and how we express ourselves and how we communicate with each other, and some group of people taught us how to speak this common language. So, if only at such a subliminal level, every person is a member of a group of people; a member of humanity, a member of God's Creation which defines, at least in part, who we are.

Virtually every human being finds their identity in something bigger than themselves. It could be as simple and subtle as being part of a group of people, as I just explained. But it is also a common human experience, all the way down (or up) through history, that there is something going on here that is much bigger than all of us put together. It seems to me that one cannot live in this Cosmos, this total Creation, without somehow becoming aware that there is some power, some force behind, if not within, everything that we call history: past, present and future. Something that made all this happen, makes all this happen, and is bringing about the future even as we speak. These common experiences and notions are the source of every religion on earth, throughout all of history.

We not only believe that there is something so much bigger than all of us put together, we also believe that we can somehow interact with this something; we can communicate with this something; we can influence this something, and that notion gives rise to each and every doctrine, dogma, ritual and religious practice of each and every religion. Ok, yes there is something much bigger than all of us which is making all of this Cosmos happen, and this is who or what it is and this is how we relate to it, communicate with, interact with and respond to what this something-bigger has told us/is telling us to do. Of course, big problems arise (and continue to arise) when any one of these religious systems assumes that they've got it all right and therefore everybody else has got it all wrong . . . but that's a topic for another sermon at another time.

You all gather here because this place is an integral part of your identity as persons; as Christians. I'm sure many of you remember being here with your grandparents, parents, brothers and sisters, friends and neighbors over a long period of time. This is indeed sacred space, and not just in being a building, but in being a place of worship, a meeting house where faith is taught, practiced and pondered, where sacred things happen, such as baptisms, confirmations, weddings, funerals; where we intentionally encounter God and celebrate our relationships with God and our responses to God and our questions to God. It is not happenchance that the word altar and alter sound so much the same. They mean the same thing: lives are changed, altered at the altar. Lives are changed just by being here. Maybe you are here because you remember how your life was changed by being here, and that is a sacred memory. Maybe you are here because you hope and believe that your life could be changed by being here and participating in this community and that is a sacred journey.

This is your congregation and I am honored to be invited to candidate for the position of your pastor. What we have in common is our identity in the common-unity that is the Church; the common union that comes with sharing our faith and life journeys with this place and this congregation as a focal point. And when we get right down to the bottom line, bedrock, nitty-gritty of it all, our common union is God as we know God in Christ.

Today we gather, in part, to celebrate Communion. Actually, every time we gather as a congregation for worship or work or just fellowship, we are celebrating our common-union, which is Christ. Today we share in a ritual; a ritual that is older than the Church itself. It comes from the last day of Jesus being here with us in person.

Jesus and his disciples had gathered to participate in their sacred ritual of Passover, when they remembered, gave thanks for and celebrated how the angel of death had passed over their people when they were enslaved in Egypt, and how if God had not made that happen they simply would not exist that day, or today. That ritual is their common-union; that which makes them one.

Jesus knew that, for all appearances, the angel of death would not pass over him this time around. He knew he was wanted by the Jewish authorities who would certainly kill him if given a chance. He knew even his closest disciples had their moments of doubt which would even lead to his betrayal. So he wanted to say goodbye in a special way; he wanted them to remember him in a ritual they would never forget. So he took some of the bread and broke it and passed it around to them saying, "This is my body, broken for you. Take and eat. Do this in remembrance of me." Then he took the wine and passed it around to them saying, "This is my blood, poured out for you. Take and drink. Do this in remembrance of me."

There are many variations on just how this ritual is presented and reenacted and after 40 something years of preparation for and service as an ordained minister I boil it all down to this:

Jesus was saying, "My friends; my disciples, I'm not going to have a body anymore, so you have to be my body. I'm not going to have any life blood anymore, so you have to be my life blood. I'm not going to be here in person to be your Christ anymore, so you have to be my person, in person; you have to be Christ to and for each other, and not just for each other, but for the whole world."

Two thousand or so years later who's he talking to? Who are the disciples gathered with him being invited to share in this ritual, not just so that we won't forget him, but that we accept the call to be Christ with and for each other? This is a daunting but joyful invitation; if not a challenge. But He wouldn't be inviting us if He didn't know we could do it.

IN THE BEGINNING . . .

Over the course of human history, dozens and dozens of stories have emerged about how and when existence came to be; how what we call Creation was created; how the earth, the heavens and all life came to be. It is a common theme in virtually every religion, even though each uses its own language, imagery and pageantry to explain how everything, including ourselves, came into being. There is also a common assumption among most religions that once upon a time, all this did not exist; once there was nothing and over time everything came to be.

We tend to somewhat derogatorily refer to these various stories as myths; Creation myths; Creation mythology. Our scientifically oriented minds want to know if something is factual, literally true, and upon finding out that it's not factually, literally true, we tend to dismiss it as something quaint, interesting, amusing, or we just throw it out the window. We do ourselves a great disservice when we throw a myth out the window. Joseph Campbell, in his wondrous book entitled, *"The Power of Myth"*, points out that every myth of every origin begins with an element of factual truth which expands into a story within which is vast amounts of meaning. From his perspective it doesn't matter whether the myth is factually, literally true. What matters is what the myth means. Take Greek mythology as a good example. We know they are not factually, literally true (even if the Greeks believed they were) but we enjoy and learn a great deal from what they mean. As I said before, our scientifically oriented minds expect, if not demand, factual, literal truth, when in reality what is important is what the story, or myth, means. And what the story or myth means is not compromised by whether or not it is factually, literally true.

I approach the Bible and the Creation stories in Genesis from this perspective. I do not judge them by whether they are factually, literally true. I embrace them for what they mean. If you come down to factual, literal truth, the ancestors of the ancient Hebrews envisioned the Cosmos as being a universe of water, and in the midst of this water God set an upside down bowl (the firmament) and blew a bubble of God's own breath into it. On the flat surface of the underside of the bowls rim, God created dry land. Then God put the sun and the moon and the stars (the heavens) on the inside of the bowl where they moved in their daily and seasonal cycles. And God shaped the dry land into mountains and valleys and rivers and lakes, and on them and in them God created all living beings. That is what the ancient Hebrews believed; all that was factually, literally true to them. Even the most ardent biblical literalist would probably not agree that such was all true, but to them, and to me, and hopefully to us, whether or not such a concept is true does not detract from what the story means, which is quite simply this: God created the heavens and the earth.

It doesn't matter to me whether it took six days, or one day (both accounts are right there in Genesis) or if it took sixteen billion years (which is cosmology's present assumption). What matters is that we believe to the point of knowing that God made it all happen; God did the creating, and more importantly, God didn't just make it happen sometime in the past; God is making it happen right here and now. God didn't do this creating just at some point in the past, when time and space and matter and energy came into being. God creating and God's creation is a work in progress. We are in the midst of God's creating; we are an integral part of God's ongoing creation.

I do not entertain any tension between science and my faith. Tension is created when one side says my interpretation is right and so every other interpretation is wrong. Science assumes it relies on factually, literal proven data in order to come to its conclusions and make its pronouncements, but science itself is a work in progress. New data and information are being discovered every day, disproving old conclusions and opening the door to new conclusions. People used to believe that the earth was a flat disk surrounded by water and the sun, moon, planets and everything else rotated around us. Even when we caught on that the earth is a sphere, we still believed that everything rotated around us. Even when we figured out that we orbit the sun, we believed that the sun was the center of the universe. So now we know that our teeny tiny planet orbits one relatively small sun in the midst of billions of other suns and solar systems that make up our galaxy, which is just one galaxy in the midst of billions of other galaxies. But none of that deters me, in any way, from believing to the point of knowing that God is doing the creating: past, present and future.

I said earlier that once there was nothing and over time everything came to be. I have no issues between evolution and my faith. The evidence is overwhelming that the whole cosmos evolved over billions of years, and life on our planet evolved over millions of years. I do not find any conflict between that evidence and my faith. If anything I find my faith enhanced by the notion of evolution. God created and God creates and evolution is how God makes it happen. Most importantly the point is that evolution is still happening; God is still creating. I simply cannot accept the Age of Enlightenment assertion that everything came to be all at once and humanity is God's crowning, perfect achievement, at least white western Europeans were God's crowning achievement, and every other kind of persons deserved to be subdued, oppressed, enslaved or just eliminated. One does not have to be a scholarly student of human history to know full well that humanity could use a good dose of further evolution. I have hope in my faith that God is making that happen, and as we observe and experience the beginnings of a global community and a global economy, I see God at work creating and re-creating. This should not be threatening; this is good news!

When I was a young boy I was taught that God was a big, old man, with long white hair and a long white beard who lived up in heaven, which I envisioned was on a cloud somewhere. When we sent rockets into space and didn't find heaven, I began to wonder . . . When I contemplated how God created male and female persons, I began to wonder why God was exclusively a male character . . . When I contemplated how God existed as a person in one place separate from every other place, I began to wonder how God could know everything about everywhere all the time . . . I embrace the notion of evolution in terms of my faith because I have found that my faith has been evolving over time. As I studied Church and doctrinal histories I realized that our awareness of God, our perception of God and our relation with God has evolved over time, and in all cases is still evolving. Nobody has God all figured out, though some would like to think they do.

On the last day in my last class at seminary, I commented to my theology professor: "You have taught me well many different theologies. So let me ask you, which one is right?" She smiled, thought for a moment, and said, "None of them. Theology, like everything else, is a work in progress, and it's up to people like you to keep searching and contribute something to the ongoing conversation." I have taken that very seriously in my ministry over the years.

I am not afraid to call a myth a myth because I am not afraid to see through a myth to what it means and build on that meaning. I am not worried about how long it took for Creation to become what it is today because I know God is made it happen, and even more so, God is making it happen right now, and God is shaping the future right before our eyes.

In the beginning God created the heavens and the earth and all living beings. Right here and now God is creating the heavens and the earth and every living thing. The future will be God's creation also. In that truth I find great hope, great peace and great faith.

Creator, creating and loving God, we open ourselves to you in prayer, to share our joys and concerns, and to listen for your still, small voice in the silence.

Once upon a time we were taught that the world is a foul and evil place, and our only hope was to go to a much better place when we die. That notion, that doctrine simply does not stand up in light of the wonder and beauty, the variety and diversity that make up the entire cosmos and our little place in it. Our coming into being in creation is not an original sin, it is an original blessing. Help us be ever mindful of that in a glorious sunrise or sunset, the lush fullness of abundant life in so many forms in Summer, the explosions of brilliant colors and the abundance of ripe fruits and vegetables in Autumn as life returns to the earth to rest, the crystalline beauty of a snowfall in Winter while plants prepare for a new beginning, the true miracle of rebirth as plants and animals emerge from their hibernations ready to explode in flowers and buds and birth. Help us ever mindful of this original, miraculous, ongoing blessing as we welcome new persons into our world, as we share our life experiences with them to help them grow and as we share our wisdom with them as our years advance.

Help us be ever mindful that all of this, ourselves included is a true miracle of epic proportions. Creation didn't have to be this way; Creation didn't have to be at all, but you in your wondrous, abundant, all encompassing love make it happen in every instant of every day of every year.

We pray for all who are unable to share in this joy due to illness, injury, maladies of body, heart, mind and soul, and make us mindful of their need for our help and healing, and our presence with them.

We each have our prayers we want to share with you, and we also need a little time to just listen. Amen.

In Spirit and In Truth

Spirituality and discussions about and experiences in the spirit, in spirituality, are not very common in the Congregational tradition, as well as many of the older, more staid Protestant traditions going back a long way, as well as most manifestations of the "Orthodox" Christian Churches going back centuries. There are some reasons for this, most of which I don't agree with. So I want to share with you this piece of history about Christian spiritually because as you will find out, discovering and practicing Christian spirituality is a big part of my repertoire, and hopefully will become part of ours . . .

Back in New Hampshire, I lived and served a Church in a little town called Canterbury which was home to one of the last vestiges of the once thriving communities called the "United Society of Believers in Christ's Second Appearance"; better known as the Shakers. They were one of a few groups of "charismatic Christians" that formed in England during the latter part of the 1700's primarily in response to the ever increasing rigidity and dominance of the Episcopal Church; the Church of England, which, even after the Reformation still seemed altogether too "catholic". One of their objections was that common worship involved no experiences of the Spirit. One just sat there and went through the rituals without feeling anything at all. On their own they had come to experience the charisma; the excitement; the ecstasy of finding a sense of truly experiential spiritual encounters with God and Christ in singing and dancing and twirling to the point that they went into a trance and collapsed undergoing sometimes violent shaking (hence their name), to awaken to relate their experiences of the presence of the Spirit of God in their life during this charismatic, ecstatic encounter with the Spirit.

Now this didn't set too well with the powers that be in the Church of England. As much as the Church of England had broken with the Roman Church in the political arena, for all practical purposes they had retained the basic premise that the Roman Church had maintained for centuries. A person cannot experience God on their own. One has to go through the Church and receive from the Priest an awareness of the presence of God through the doctrine, dogma and ritual of the Church. This had been the essential doctrine of the Church for better than 1500 years at that point. And though the Church of England claimed to be "reformed" they hung on to that essential, hierarchical chain of command for dear life. And along comes a small group of people who claim that each and every person can have their own personal experience of the Spirit of God, and they do so in their ecstatic "shaking", which they relate back to their community, and in which they all share as a community.

It wasn't long before this little community came under terrible persecution by the English authorities and it wasn't long after that when they booked passage to America where they hoped they would find the religious freedom they yearned for. The established Congregational Church of the time initially welcomed them, but when they learned of the true nature of their religious experiences, they persecuted them too. Though the Shaker community was slowly growing, they were constantly on the run for their lives. Many were beaten, some were killed, even Mother Ann, the original founder of the Shaker community was imprisoned and later died at an early age primarily because of the persecutions and abuse she had endured.

So the Shakers developed their own strategy for surviving in a hostile world. They gave up trying to establish themselves within existing communities, and they set out to establish their own communities. There was lots of open space at the time so this was practical and possible. The first settlement was in Niskayuna, NY, northwest of Albany, and by the time of their heyday they had dozens of communities throughout New England and west to Ohio and Tennessee housing thousands of Shakers.

At the heart of the Shaker tradition are the words "Hands to work and Hearts to God." That was the practical application of their spiritual beliefs and experiences. There was no distinction between work and faith, between worship and daily life. I had the privilege of getting to know the last two Shaker Eldresses and the one remaining Sister at the Canterbury Shaker village and one day I asked one of the Eldresses how they celebrated communion. Her response was quick and to the point: "Oh, you mean that thing you do with bread and wine? We had no rituals like that. Our very lives were our communion with Christ and God."

The Shakers never published any doctrines and dogmas, or their own Theology or Book of Worship. Their relationships with God and Christ were essentially personal and even more essentially spiritual. To try to pin down and define just what they believed and how they worshipped was out of the question. Their primary concern was that their faith was lived out every day in their life together. Everybody in the community had a job that they chose because they believed that one's job was one's calling. Young people were encouraged to try out different jobs so they could end up in one they really liked and felt called to. There were no distinctions between men's jobs and women's jobs. A woman could be a carpenter or a stone mason if she chose and felt called to, and a man could be a cook or a seamster if he chose and felt called to, and if at some stage in their life one wanted to change jobs, that too was encouraged. They were incredibly creative and innovative. They invented dozens of tools and practices, from the circular saw blade, to the clothespin, to the flat broom, to packaging and selling vegetable and flower seeds, and of course, their wondrously simple, elegant and functional furniture and cabinetry, and they did not patent any of it. Everything they created or invented was their gift to the community and more so to the whole world, even their poetry and prose and songs. Maybe a person created something, but that was the Spirit working through them; there was no question of taking personal credit for it or owning it or personally owning anything, for that matter. We have all heard the Shaker tune "Simple Gifts" used in everything from the Broadway production "River Dance" to background music for car sales.

Above all they were totally generous and giving. One of the reasons that the communities grew so fast and furiously was that everybody, and I do mean everybody and anybody was welcomed into a Shaker community as long as they put their 'Hands to work and their hearts to God.' In their time the Shaker communities were havens against a precarious and often hostile world. They attracted people of all walks of life, especially children. The two Eldresses I knew had come to the Shaker village as young children because their parents couldn't afford to take care of them. But not everybody in a Shaker community was by definition a Shaker. Some people came just for the winter or until they found a new direction in life. When a young person turned eighteen they were given the choice of "signing the covenant" or going on their way. If a person "signed the covenant" they were a Shaker for life.

Mother Ann prophesied that the day would come when the Shakers would dwindle to just a handful, but the work would go on, and if the Shakers ever ceased to be there would be a new manifestation of the second coming of Christ. Today there is just one remaining Shaker community in Sabbath Day Lake, Maine with only a handful of members. One of the basic tenets of the Shakers was that they were celibate; they had no children of their own, but they openly and freely served all the children of their world. Over time the world became healthier, safer and more prosperous. The world came to not need the Shakers anymore.

The Shakers believed that their community was the second coming of Christ, and they arrived at that conclusion not by following some set in stone doctrines and dogmas, but by opening themselves to personal and communal experiences in the Spirit of God. Again, for centuries the Church had proclaimed the doctrine that a person could not come to or have a personal, spiritual relationship with God by themselves, but only through the teaching, the doctrines and the dogmas of the Church. If people had a spiritual encounter or relationship with God they pretty much kept it to themselves, let alone shared it as an integral part of their community. There are many examples of a person publically claiming to have had a personal, spiritual encounter with God, and they ended up being burned at the stake as a blasphemous heretic.

So there is historical reason why we shy away from pursuing or sharing our spiritual experiences, but the Good News is we all have them. It doesn't mean we have to go into frenzy or a trance and fall down shaking. The presence of the Spirit of God is, I believe, much more subtle than that. I believe each and all have spiritual encounters with God in many ways, at many times. Search your hearts, I bet you know of your own spiritual encounters with God; your own spirituality.

One of the problems with spiritual experiences is that they tend to be rather emotional. When I was back in seminary the rule of the game was theo-logical; God is logical and our understandings about God MUST be logical too. There is no room for emotion in expressing our understanding of and relationship with God. So we tend to shy away from our spirituality and our emotions in our worship of God and in our personal and communal relations with God.

The Good News is that we can be free to have and share our spiritual experiences and I encourage us all to do so. After all, it is the Spirit of God making it all happen.

Our God, we may not be able to see you face to face, because we know you don't have a face like we do, but we know that you are as close and all encompassing as the very air we breathe . . . we ask you to breathe on us because the word Spirit comes from the word for breath, air, wind . . . we may not able to see your breath, your Spirit, but we can certainly feel it . . . so often we only try to understand you and wrap you up in neat little theo-logical boxes: books of logical reasoning by which we attempt to explain you: who and what you are and what you ask of us and offer to us, but the truth is that you are so much more than that and you are not bound by the limits of our reasoning and logic . . . we know you are everywhere and every when . . . your Spirit permeates the entire cosmos from tiniest particle to the whole eternal and infinite universe . . . from the furthest away places to the deepest recesses of our very beings . . . you are always there, you are always here, you are always above us, below us, in front of us, behind us, next to us and most importantly within us and among us . . . help us become very mindful of your presence; help us learn to listen to your presence; help us learn to experience your presence; help our spirits be open to your spirit that we can learn and share ever more fully the infinite and eternal love you pour out on each of us, all of us together, and all of Creation . . . let the Spirit of your love fill us and flow through us in everything we do.

We pray that your Spirit will bring help and healing, strength and stamina, patience and tolerance, comforts and joy to all who are in such need due to illness or injury in body, mind, heart, soul, in ourselves and in our relationships . . . and that's just about all of us. Help us all be free to call out for your help and blessings when and as we need them, because we don't just know you are here, we know if we open ourselves up to you we can feel and be filled with your Spirit: the source of all our spirits and our spirit together. Amen.

ONE GOD . . . MANY NAMES

My earliest memories of anything and everything have to do with the Church. My earliest friendships were established there and continued right up through High School and beyond in some cases. Even though they were involved in many other activities, the Church was the center of the lives of my parents and the rest of my family. Rather than say that I was "taught" the Church, it's more honest to say I "caught" the Church. As I gradually became aware of and participated in the teachings and practices of the Church, it became the center of my being, where it remains today. But it has not always been smooth sailing through all these years. Even as I got more and more personally involved in the Church, and wrestled with all the tides of raging adolescence against the rather strict morality of the Church, and I began to encounter conflicting and contradicting teachings within the Church, I amassed quite a collection deep-seated questions, some of which I was afraid to ask out loud because I had been taught that they just might go against the grain of Church teachings. Even in the throes of Seminary diatribes, debates and discussions, there were some questions that still nagged at me. Even after I was ordained (or maybe more so because I was ordained) it took many years for me to finally give the big question voice.

In retrospect the question seems rather obvious and straight forward, and I'm not sure why I was so afraid of asking it. So I will openly and honestly share this question with all of you. If there indeed is only one God, why are there so many religions? If there indeed is only one God, why are so many of these religions wracked with internal disputes, as well be in dire conflict with each other? If there is indeed only one God, does that mean that only one of these different religions is right and all the rest are wrong? There is no doubt that many if not most of the world's religions assume that about themselves: they are right and everybody else is wrong, and aside from lukewarm attempts at ecumenical cooperation and tolerance among the denominations within any one religion, there has traditionally been very little effort put in to trying to truly understand each other's religion on the grand scale, let alone learn from each other. How and what could a Christian learn from a Jew, a Muslim, a Buddhist, a Hindu, a Native American, etc., and back and forth, in and out among any and all of them?

Over the course of the last couple of decades many individuals and groups of people have begun to ask these questions and take them very seriously, and these people are not just a bunch of new age transcendentalists or tree huggers or flower worshipers. Most are very serious and respected scholars and religious leaders, and I consider myself to be one of their students. The question at the heart of the matter remains the same: if there is indeed only one God, why are there so many so often conflicting religions? An answer begins to take shape when one considers that the problem is not whether or not there is indeed only one God, who we know by many names. The problem is that each religion has a different perception of this one God, and like the blind people and the elephant, each insists that their perception is the only one that is right. In a nutshell, the problem isn't with God: the problem is with religion.

I had the wonderful opportunity to lead the House of Abraham house builds when I was with Habitat for Humanity, in which Christians, Muslims and Jews worked together to build a house. We took this as an opportunity to learn about each other and in doing so learn from each other. It immediately became obvious that we have a lot to learn about each other and there is also a lot we can learn from each other. In one case we were asked to share any rules or laws pertaining to food that were in our religions. The Jews explained the traditions of their kosher laws. The Muslims explained the traditions of their cleanliness laws. And when we Christians were asked about our food and/or cleanliness laws, we looked at each other blankly and said simply, "Except for the cleansing rite of Baptism, we don't have any." Everybody laughed in a good way, but it left me thinking that it might not be a bad idea of we Christians thought a little more about what we eat and take the advice of "wash your hands" a little more seriously. These laws did not come into being out of a vacuum. They arose from very practical experiences. Centuries before anybody ever heard of trichinosis it was observed that people could get really sick and die from eating pork. Centuries before anybody knew about bacteria it was observed that people tended to get sick and die if they didn't wash their food and their hands before they ate.

One stumbling block we did encounter in the House of Abraham projects was trying to find a time when we all could work together. People worked so weekdays were mostly out. Friday is the Muslim Sabbath, Saturday is the Jewish Sabbath and Sunday is (supposed to be) the Christian Sabbath, and though individually people of all three faiths admitted they tended not to take the Sabbaths as seriously as some orthodox groups do and they were willing to work on any day, the powers that be (the Muslim coalition and the Jewish coalition) that were organizing all of this could not openly condone their people not observing their Sabbath, and we knew it was not wise to subvert the powers that be. It ended up, for the most part, that we worked on Sunday because we Christians didn't have any power-that-be to answer to. But it left me wondering if it might do we Christians well to more seriously consider a weekly day of rest and rejuvenation.

We have a lot to learn about each other and from each other, and the need for us to do so becomes increasingly important just about every day. The paths of history are log-jammed with the bloody results of one religion insisting they have an exclusive on the Truth and everybody else is wrong, and not only between religions. The paths of history are log-jammed with the bloody results of various denominations within a given religion insisting they have an exclusive on the truth: Protestants against Catholics, Jew against Jew, Muslim against Muslim, Hindu against Hindu etc., etc., etc.

At the core of virtually every religion is the belief that there is one God, one Deity, one driving force and one ultimate goal, who we know by many names, and if we take that notion as seriously as we should we quickly come to the conclusion that our problem is not with the one God, but within and among our various perceptions of this one God and how we express and live out our perceptions. We express our perceptions in our doctrines and dogmas, and it's the differences between our doctrines and dogmas that get us in trouble. What it all boils down to for me is that what happens is that we end up worshipping our doctrines and dogmas more than we worship the one God, and by worshipping I don't mean just ritual recitations and meditations, but how we live out our very lives.

At the core of virtually every religion is also the belief that this one God is essentially loving, even though that central belief is often rendered down to the assertion that this one God only loves those who worship God the way "we" do. Again, that is our doctrines and dogmas getting in the way of the love of this one God. I have come to the conclusion that any religion that claims to perceive one loving God, yet condones if not promotes if not perpetrates oppression and violence against anyone else is, quite simply, wrong.

What remains is the Truth that there is just one, loving God, Creator, Sustainer and Lover of all that is, has being and has life. We Christians come to know this one, loving God through Christ, whom we know to be God incarnate. When we get to know Christ, we are getting to know God. Christ says, "I am the way, the truth and the life . . ." and he's right. Christ/God IS the way the truth and the life, and not the doctrines and dogmas we enshrine and imprison Christ/God in. The same can happen through Mohammed if you are a Muslim, through the Torah and the Prophets if you are a Jew, through Buddha if you are a Buddhist, and on down the line. Doctrines and dogmas can lead one to the way, the truth and the life, but in the end it's what happens in here, in our hearts and minds and bodies all as one that we encounter and establish a relationship with this one God. When we allow that to happen we find that God indeed does love everybody and everything and calls us to do the same, and when we do that conflict ends and true peace begins.

I'd like share a few of my experiences with other religions and what I have learned from them. I like to say that a Buddhist finally taught me how to pray. We were discussing prayer and a friend observed that we Christians (and others) tend to approach prayer as if we were delivering a shopping list to God in a basically one sided conversation. He said what I had to do was shut up and listen, which is basically what the Buddhists do in meditation. Go ahead, say your piece, but then take the time to quiet yourself; to shut up and listen. I like to say that a Native American taught me how to finally see Creation as the blessing that it is; that the cosmos is a living thing and we are an integral and responsible part of this cosmos. We have no right to oppress or destroy Creation, including every living thing in it. I like to say that a Muslim taught me what it is like to envision a religion in which there is no doctrine of original sin; where Creation is the original blessing and we are part of and responsible to that blessing.

I have great hope in the love of our one living, loving God, in whom alone I put my living faith.

Creator, Sustainer, Lover, Yahweh, Elohim, Adonai, Lord, Heavenly Father, Heavenly Mother, our God, everyone's God . . . we know you by many names, and in our words you are the one and only God who we know in and through Jesus Christ. Please help us understand, appreciate and be open to the truth that though others call you by other names and envision and depict you in different imagery and others speak about you in different words, we're all talking about the same thing: you, our God.

It is so incredibly incongruous that we argue, fight and even go to war over which name is right, which image is right, which doctrines and dogmas are right. This only goes to show that in greater scheme of things you are the only one who is right and if we could only slow down a bit, swallow our pride, see beyond our prejudices, admit that all our doctrines and dogmas are weak attempts to define you, take off our blinders, we just might get a glimpse of who you really are. What is right is to do justice, love kindness and humbly with you, by whatever name we call you. You call us to love one another as you love us: unconditionally, totally, openly, freely. Our God, help us do so in all the ways our lives touch others.

We pray that in your love you will shower help and healing on all people, in all the ways they are needed so desperately by so many and not just individually, but shower your help and healing on our families, our communities, our nations and our world. Help us heal and be healed by truly knowing that you indeed our one, loving God.

We know you by many names, and you know our names, each and every one of us . . . hear us and help us listen to you as we share our prayers in silence.

The Art Of Living

God is infinitely and eternally creative. Creation did not happen sometime in the distant past. Creation is happening right here in this ever present moment, moving through time as what we call right now. Even as Autumn sets in, the buds are formed and the seeds are planted, to sleep under the coming Winter snows until next Spring. Animals prepare throughout the Winter to give birth in the coming Spring. Even as we speak old stars and planets are dying and new stars and planets are being born throughout our universe. Even as we take in one breath at time and our hearts beat one beat at a time, old cells are being replaced with new cells. Creation is not a onetime long in the past event. Creation is constantly happening ever moving forward into the future and as we are creations of God's ongoing creation, as living creatures we are each and all endowed with an amount of our own creativity.

The key to surviving as life forms on this planet, or any who or what anywhere else, is adaptability: the ability to adapt to new situations and opportunities. The world is constantly changing, evolving, moving forward into new versions of itself. If a species is going to survive these changes it has to adapt to its new surroundings. Over the millions and millions of years in the history of life on this planet, relatively few have been able to adapt and so survive. Some have been able to evolve into new species. Some have simply ceased to exist.

The key to adaptability is the ability to be creative. We tend to rather arrogantly assume that we human critters are the only ones who are truly creative. Well, try to build a bird's nest and see how creative we are. Try to build a beaver lodge, a wasp nest, an ant hill, try to survive unclothed at the north or south poles, or in the middle of the desert, or in outer space. This is not in any way to say that we are not creative, but we should recognize that all life forms are creative in their own ways.

Obviously, we human critters are incredibly creative. From the clothes we wear, the food we eat to all the vast and amazing machines we have built, we are incredibly creative and adaptable. But we have one extension to our creativity that no other life forms seem to have and this is our ability to express ourselves as to what we feel or what we think or what we imagine. In some ways this ability builds upon our ability to communicate: to convey thoughts and feelings, ideas and imaginations directly to each other. Many life forms have some ability to communicate, some through vocalizations, some through body language, some through changing colors, but we seem to be only ones who can sit down and engage in a conversation, and not just about where the next meal might come from, or what other critters are approaching us, or whether we should run and hide or stand up and fight. We can have conversations about incredibly complex thoughts and conceptions. We can share our imaginations, our hopes and fears, our expectations. We can embrace incredibly complex mechanical and mathematical constructs and envision them and share our visions and turn them into physical realities. We are incredibly creative.

What really sets us apart from other critters, though, is that we have the ability to be self expressing. We can express who we are as individuals and communities and cultures and religions. We can express how we envision ourselves and our world and throughout human history there has been this constant driving force to do just that: to make something or do something that expresses who we are and what we believe, and the name of this unique form of communication is Art.

Why did our ancient ancestors put their hands on cave walls and spatter colored clay over them, leaving the outlines of their hands? They were simply saying I am here, later to be seen as he or she was here. They are images of themselves. Why did they paint elaborate images of animals and landscapes? They were saying this is/was our world; this is what life was all about; this is the way it is or was. Why did they paint and carve statues depicting things that obviously were not just human, but were bigger and more important than just humans: their deities, their gods, whatever they called them? They were saying this is what we believe. So why did they do all this? Because they had the driving urge if not need to express themselves about whom and what they and their world were all about. That is Art.

Obviously we had spoken languages and visual imagery long before we invented a written language and we started carving statues and painting pictures, long before we had any words to write on something. The invention of written languages opened us up to a whole new dimension of communications. We no longer were limited to images to express ourselves, we could communicate direct thoughts and feelings down through history, and in many ways written language was and still is an Art form. We use it for technical communication, but we also use it to express our deepest thoughts and feelings, who we are and how we interact with the world around us.

Once upon a time there was no distinction between formal Art and general communication. As we began to use oral and written communication for more purely technical information, there became a distinction between informal communication and true Art, but that deep seated inner need to envision and so communicate who we are and how see our world and our place in it; the need to communicate our deepest feelings about and our conceptions of God remain a driving force in many people's lives.

There is, of course the art of literature and poetry. Poetry merges with music in songs. Music stands on its own as an Art. Painting in all its forms as well as still-photography and sculpture stand on their own as Art forms. Movies and video blend together visual, musical and language arts. Occasionally architecture blends visual imagery, sculpture and practicality in an Art form. The common thread is this need to express something of oneself that goes well beyond just a written explanation of their conceptions and concerns.

Art and religion have always been very closely connected. It wasn't until the invention of the printing press that the ability to read and write became common place. For centuries before that what better way could there be to present the images of the Bible stories about God than in painting, sculpture and music? They were the common language among illiterate people who often spoke different languages. It doesn't matter what language one speaks to appreciate Michelangelo's Sistine Chapel ceiling. The ongoing dialogs and debates about God and the Bible only came about when most everyone could read and write. Unfortunately, the need for Christian Art declined as theological debate emerged. Our own Congregational tradition contributed to this decline by banning any and all iconate imagery from the sanctuary. Gone were the sculpture, paintings and, in its early days, even music and the Cross, that were such a big part of the Episcopal, Roman and other Orthodox traditions. The assumption was that all iconate imagery could lead a person to worship a statue or a painting instead of God, who by then was believed to be only accessible by theo-logical discussion and expression in doctrine and dogma, lectures and sermons. Gone were the visual, musical, scented expressions of our faith that fill a person with a wholistic experience, not just an intellectual experience.

But religious Art is by no means dead. Culturally, with Art no longer being the primary means of religious expression, the Art world has tended to become more and more secular with Art themes including multitudes of issues and concerns aside from religious concerns. With Art no longer center stage in our culture and religion, the serious work of Art has been increasingly marginalized. Artists tend to live in 'colonies', apart from the secular world, where they can indulge in their right brained endeavors without being judged by their left brained logical, rational, reasonable compatriots. Artists tend to live apart . . . I choose to live within a wonderful community like ours . . . and preach and teach and live our faith . . . even as an Artist.

Art is very much center stage in my life, both appreciating it and creating it. I am quite serious about my wood turnings as Art, as well as my photography and poetry. I am also quite convinced that each and every person is in their own way an artist, or at least they could be with some encouragement. Unfortunately, most of our educational systems do not make Art a priority. At the heart of the matter is the truth that one cannot teach Art; one cannot teach Creativity. Giving a child a coloring book and demanding that they 'stay within the lines' teaches neither art nor Creativity. Telling a person to make as close a copy of a painting as possible may well teach technique, but not creativity. One can only encourage a person to reach inside and release the creative forces that they are created with. This is a holy and spiritual act.

Often when I suggest to someone that every person has the potential to be an Artist, I am met with. "Waddya mean? I can't paint like Michelangelo." No of course you can't, you're not Michelangelo, but you might be able to paint from yourself. "Waddya mean? I can't make music like Beethoven." "Waddya mean? I can't write like Shakespeare." No, of course you can't, you're not Beethoven or Shakespeare, but you might be able to make music or write from yourself, and on and on and on. We all have experiences that could and would be best expressed in an Art form that goes well beyond just a logical verbal explanation.

So why is Carl presenting a sermon about Art, you may be asking? Well, as I said at the beginning, our Creator, our God bestows on each one us our own measure of Creativity, which may come in many forms, some very practical and some unique and individual, but this Creativity will never be realized until it is released. Our Creativity is a God given gift and it's never too late to let it out, to let it come to life.

I hope as time goes here to offer some workshops in Creativity, so we can get a glimpse of our Creativity that waits to be awakened.

Our God, our Father, our Mother, our Brother and Sister, our Friend and our ever present Companion . . . our Creator who from nothing has created and continues to create everything, here and now, past and present, who leads us into your future . . . we acknowledge that you have endowed each and every one of us with a touch of your creativity, an inkling of your eternal and infinite creative love . . . and we also acknowledge that we have used our abilities to do some wondrous things, to make life so much better for so many people . . . but we also confess that, in our history, we have used our creativity in ways that oppress, harm, hurt and destroy so many people.

We want to be able to share our words, our thoughts, our visions, our hopes and our fears, we want to share in our creativity so that we continue to help make life better for ourselves and each other . . . help us be mindful of the creativity you endow us with that we can do so . . . help us be free to express this creativity in any and ways that we can . . . help us paint beautiful pictures that praise your creation . . . help us make beautiful music that praises the sound of your name . . . help us be the creative creatures you have created us to be. Amen.

For the Love of God

When I was back in Seminary I learned a whole lot of things about a whole lot of things: Biblical interpretation, eschatology, hermeneutics, ethics and a whole slew of different theo-logical interpretations, most of which I couldn't rattle off today if I tried. What has endured the most and has served me the best over the years is my knowledge of Biblical Hebrew and Greek. One class of either was all that was required, but I ended up taking two classes in each. At the time I could pick up something in Hebrew or Greek and read it off like it was the Sunday news. That talent has faded, but what has not faded is my ability to take a Bible verse, track it down in its original language and attempt to make a more accurate translation than what shows up in our various Bibles.

Some ask "Why bother? Why don't you just trust what other translators have already done?" That's because our various English Bibles often have very different wording for the same passages, and when I want to know what is closest to being accurate I go back to the original text in its original language, and that is not always an easy thing to do. The bottom line reality of languages is that they are not static or interchangeable. Rarely do we find a situation where what is said in one language is literally translatable to another. Among the Western European languages that derive from Latin, this is not such a big issue because we all start with the same basic world views that are the foundations for Latin.

A language does not just express what we think. A language defines how we think. We think in English with all our basic assumptions about the reality of the world we live in, all of which are expressed in our thoughts and our words, most of which can be relatively easily translated into or from languages like Spanish or French because we all have a common basic conception of the nature of reality. Things change dramatically when you encounter a very different language with a very different conception of the nature of reality.

In the Biblical world, what we call the Old Testament was originally spoken and then written in Hebrew. As Jews Jesus and the people around him all understood Hebrew, but their common language was Aramaic. This Aramaic was translated into and written in Greek. Everything we know about what Jesus said and did was originally expressed in Aramaic, which was translated into Greek. Paul and everyone after him in the New Testament spoke and wrote only in Greek. The issue is that Hebrew and Aramaic are very ancient and very different languages from anything like English. Greek is not so much of a problem because Greek evolved into Latin which, again, evolved into the languages of Western Europe where our English comes from.

The problem is that, again, one language is rarely directly translatable into another, and when one encounters a language that is as foreign and different as Hebrew or Aramaic it can be very difficult if not sometimes impossible to effectively or accurately translate the basic concepts of those languages into English. This ambiguity opens up plenty of room for widely varying interpretations of what a certain passage might mean, and so there is lots of room for varying, if not often conflicting, "translations" of the same passage. It also leaves plenty of room for the translators to insert their own agendas in how they phrase their "translation".

So before everybody nods off to sleep, I'll get right to a prime example of how what I am talking about works and this prime example is the phrases that include ". . . the fear of the Lord . . ." A few examples are:

Ps. 19:9: "The fear of the Lord is clean and endures forever."
Ps. 111:10: "The fear of the Lord is the beginning of wisdom."
Ecc. 12:13: "Let us hear the conclusion of the whole matter: Fear the Lord and keep his commandments: for this is the whole duty of man."

. . . and there are dozens more to choose from.

My problem is that with all the multitudes of expressions of the love, grace, steadfastness, justice and faithfulness of God in Christ, where does this notion of ". . . the fear of the Lord . . ." come from? Are we supposed to be afraid of God? So I dig out my Hebrew resources and say let's take a look at what is being said here in Hebrew, and the first thing that comes to light is the phrase "the Lord . . ." Every time you see the phrase "the Lord . . . 'in the Old Testament, the Hebrew word that is being translated is God's name: Yahweh. Now Hebrew is kind of unique in that Hebrew is written only using consonants without vowels. The consonants that appear as the name of God are essentially YHWH. It was also a long standing tradition among the Hebrew people that one never, ever speaks the name of God. They would say something roughly equivalent to "the Lord . . ." So having never spoken the word that comes with YHWH, nobody knows for certain what the vowels were that go with YHWH. It is commonly accepted by Jewish and other Hebrew scholars that the vowels most likely are YaHWeH: Yahweh, but nobody knows for absolute certain. To illustrate the room for ambiguity in all of this, traditional interpreters of the Bible, like King James scholars and the Jehovah Witnesses, take the YHWH and translate them as JHVH, which ends up as Jehovah. Go figure!

So what it all boils down to for me is that "YHWH" and ". . . the Lord . . ." all refer to the same thing: God, so why not just translate that word as "God". So now we have ". . . the fear of God . . ." and the question is what "fear" means. The Hebrew word that gets translated into "fear" includes many other nuances besides being afraid of something or someone like one would be afraid of a mean person. Probably the clearest translation would be something like "reverence", "awe and respect", something like that, but certainly not "fear". ". . . reverence for God . . ." certainly takes on meaning that is much more compatible with the love and grace of God we find in Christ than "fear". So let's take another look at those passages:

Ps. 19:9: "Reverence for God is clean and endures forever."
Ps. 111:10: "Reverence for God is the beginning of wisdom."
Ecc. 12:13: "Let us hear the conclusion of the whole matter: Revere God and keep God's commandments: for this is the whole duty of humanity."

Our relationship with God is not based on fear. There certainly are many references to the anger and wrath of God in the Old Testament, but they fade away when we are introduced to the love and grace of God in Christ. Our relationship with God is based on God's love for us. God pours out God's love and grace on us hoping that we will respond to God by loving God, which means doing what God hopes we will do, which is to pour out our love and grace on each other.

So maybe I'm stretching the point, but let's take one more look at those passages:

Ps. 19:9: "Love of God is clean and endures forever."
Ps. 111:10: "Love of God is the beginning of wisdom."
Ecc. 12:13: "Let us hear the conclusion of the whole matter: Love God and keep God's commandment (which is to love one another): for this is the whole duty of humanity."

Once upon a time fear was the prime factor in how the Church expressed what a person's relationship with God should be. If one did not follow the doctrines and dogmas of the Church one could not receive "the medicine of immortality" which is what they called the Eucharist; what we now call simply communion. If one did not follow the doctrines and dogmas of the Church to the letter, thus one could not receive the "medicine of immortality", thus one certainly lived in fear of an afterlife in hell, and that fear was the foundation of one's faith.

For the love of God, and by the love of God, those days are long gone. One of the phrases we hear many times in the Gospels and the later writings is "Be not afraid . . ." Let us hear those words and not be afraid as we approach this table, and know that what we are offered here is an outpouring of God's love and grace, and God hopes for the same from us to each other in return. "For the love of God, be not afraid . . ."

Our loving and gracious God, you know us and understand us and love us no matter what language we speak. You understand each and every one of us even when we can't understand each other. You give us ears to hear with, voices to speak with, minds that are ever seeking to better understand and express our perceptions and conceptions through speaking and writing, but so often we become bound by our limitations and our prejudices: we want to be convinced that we've got it right, even if that implies that everybody else doesn't.

Paul says so eloquently, "(now) we know only in part, and we prophesy only in part; but when the complete comes, the partial will come to an end . . . For now we see in a mirror dimly, but then we will see face to face . . . Now I know only in part; then I will know fully, even as I have been fully known."

Help us open our hearts and minds to the truth that we have a lot to learn from each other . . . help us open our hearts and minds to you and your infinite and eternal love and grace . . . help us be open to the fact that our minds cannot encompass you and certainly cannot contain or define you . . . help us be open to your language, your vision, your wisdom; the power of the presence of your love and grace.

We all need your help and healing in many ways: in body, heart, mind and spirit. Pour out your healing love on each and every one of us that we made be made whole by your grace. Amen.

Goin Home

Everybody wants to have a home. Most all of us do, but some of us have lost our homes, either literally or figuratively, or never found a home. "Home" is usually fashioned after the place we grew up in and the people we grew up with, and if that home was safe and secure and nurturing that is the kind of home we go looking for or attempt to recreate. If home was not that way, we will meet people along the way who had or have a home like that and we find ourselves yearning for that safety, security and nurturing; we yearn for a home.

I have a few friends back in Farmington who still live the houses they grew up in, and their closest friends and companions are the people they grew up with. As a Pastor I have lived a pretty nomadic life style. My family and I lived in many different houses in many different communities, so "home" was not so much a specific place as it was the people we were as a family. We sort of carried our home around in a big backpack and when we got to a new place we set up our home again. And when our marriage fell apart we had to create two homes, where our children could still find that safety, security and nurturing they were used to.

So home is not so much a place as it is a family; a community. A home is a collection of relationships that give us safety, security and nurturing. A home is not a static thing. It is a living thing, and all homes have good times and tough times, but that mutual commitment to safety, security and nurturing; that love, is what holds a home together and keeps it alive and growing.

There's a great old saying: "Home is where the heart is." and that is profoundly true. At the heart of the matter is the truth that before a house becomes a home, or even before a collection of relationships becomes a home, a home is something deep within us that comes out of us to become a home. I believe "home" is a universal yearning that we are created with and endowed with. Another way of putting it is that home is a universal yearning for love: to receive and give love, and this yearning for and searching for and the innate need to share this love come from the love of our Creator; our God.

When times are good we tend to take that goodness for granted, and we just might well wander off like Prodigal children. But when times are tough, we want to go home. When we have to deal with tough times like illness, injury, grief, worry and uncertainty, we just want to go home, and God welcomes us home with open arms and a grand celebration. The Church is called and empowered by God to be just that home, not just like an Ozzie and Harriet, Leave it to Beaver sort of idyllic American nuclear family (though they are ultimately important for the nurturing of children), but as a community of God lovers who are called and empowered to love one another as God loves them. That is who we are called and empowered to be . . . let us do . . . let us make a home with an open loving door.

The 23rd Psalm sums it up, if we love one another as we are loved by God, "Surely goodness and mercy shall follow us all the days of our lives, we shall dwell in the Home of God, forever."

Creator God, Sustaining God, living, loving all wondrous God, we thank you for all the ways we know what it is to be at home, in a home, to work together to create and maintain a home. You pour out on us the loving help and healing that we endeavor to manifest in our own homes. Your life and your love are both the sources and the goal of our life and love within and among us.

Help us realize this love, this safety, this security, this nourishing in our own homes, in our extended homes, and in our home here in your Church. Help us stock up on our love and compassion so that when people come in our open doors we are ready and willing to truly be your servants, one to another; we are ready and willing to be Christ to all whom come here.

We pray for all the ways we yearn for and need a home, where help and healing happen spontaneously, where ill and injured bodies, hearts, minds and spirits find the rest and rejuvenation we all need in one way or many. You are our one true Pastor, and we are your people . . . make your presence known within us and among us every minute of every day . . . that we may be empowered to the same for others.

We need quiet time both to share the joys and concerns of our hearts with you . . . and we need time to stop and listen to the sound of your still, small voice. Amen.

You Gotta Serve Somebody

The people of Israel had finally made it: they were home. They had conquered the native peoples and claimed all the land of Canaan as their own, now calling it Israel. They had escaped from slavery under the Egyptians. They had survived wandering in the wilderness for forty years, and now, as Joshua recounts, they were established in a land that was not their own and they were living in houses that they had not built. But they believed that they were home and at the heart of the matter was their belief, their faith that God had done all this for them. They had come through the worst of times and they were just beginning what they believed would be the best of times. Instead of strutting his stuff like a proud conqueror and playing up his successful leadership at making all this happen, Joshua defers to God and gives the people a very stern warning and demands of them a very clear choice. "Choose this day who you will serve."

It is a very common human characteristic that when we are going through the worst of times we do a whole lot more praying than when we're going through the best of times, no matter who or what we are praying to. The people of Israel had prayed their way out of Egypt. They had prayed their way through the wilderness and into Canaan, and by all accounts their prayers had been answered. They were home. The best was yet to come and the best was just beginning. And it's right at that point that Joshua admonishes the people: Don't forget how this all came to be. Don't forget that once upon a time you were slaves and now you are free. Don't forget that once you were homeless; that you were strangers in a strange land, and now you are home. Don't forget that all of this is not your own doing, but it is all indeed a gift from God. He was telling them, warning them not to take the good times for granted because they might well not last, and, most of all don't assume that you made the good times happen all happen all by yourself. And when the worst of times come around again, don't blame God, because you probably played a big role in bringing about the worst of times all by yourself. Don't forget to thank God for the good times when they are happening. Choose this day whom you will serve, and if it's not God, watch out!

I don't usually wax as legalistic as this scripture might appear and I want to assure you that I do not take the blessing and blame game so simplistically. I also have to say that it is sometimes not so easy to extrapolate on words that were spoken to a certain people at a certain time in a certain context long, long, long ago and apply them to the present we people are living in. Joshua was speaking to the people of Israel, admonishing them to serve the Lord; to serve their one God, Yahweh, in a time when there were many, many other gods to choose from. In Christ and throughout our Christian tradition we maintain that there is only one God, though that has and does put us at odds with others who believe the same thing: that there is only one God, but others give this one God other names and interpret God's words and actions in different ways. Just take a look at the middle-east to understand that phenomenon. Even within our own culture most all of us would assume that there is only one God, even though among ourselves we have widely differing and often conflicting interpretations as to what this God is all about.

So, yes, we would all say that there is only one God, but that, to be honest, is not all that true; at least that is not how we carry on our lives. We might well say that there is only one (capital G) God, but we surround ourselves with lots of lesser (small g) gods which we have to serve and answer to, and the names of these gods are social, political, economic, cultural and even religious institutions. By (small g) gods I am talking about forces, principalities, institutions that shape our lives, define our lives, control our lives and we have to answer to them. We have to engage these forces in a relationship of servitude, whether we want to or not. Try not paying your taxes and see who's really in charge here. Try not paying the interest on your bills and loans and see who's really in charge here. We pray to God to forgive our debts as we forgive our debtors. Try laying that one on your Bank or the IRS and see what happens.

I often find myself in conversations that go something like this. Do you believe in the Bible? I answer: No, I don't believe in the Bible, but I do believe in the God that the Bible is talking about. Do you believe in Christ? I answer: In as much as we believe that Christ is God incarnate, yes, but more to the point I believe in the God that

Christ is talking about. Do you believe in religion? I answer: No, I don't believe in religion, per se, but I do believe in the God that my religion is talking about. Do you believe in the Church? I answer: No, I don't believe in the Church, but I do believe in the God who calls the Church into being. When I honestly reply to the question: Do you believe in God? I have to say that the issue is not so much whether or not I believe **IN** God, but that I **BELIEVE** God.

For me believing **IN** God is the first step in coming to **BELIEVE** God. If one is wondering whether or not to believe in God, what the person is really asking is whether or not God exists. If a person believes that God exists, the issue is not whether or not one believes **IN** God, but whether or not they **BELIEVE** God. Of course this rather simplistic sounding formula becomes incredibly cloudy and complex when one has to choose among the multitudes of interpretations of God that are floating around out there to find one that they can honestly say they **BELIEVE.**

When somebody asks me if I am a Christian I have to honestly respond by asking: What do you mean by that? There are many interpretations of what it means to believe God that I simply cannot agree with. At many times in my life I have had conversations with an atheist in which I ask them what God or what kind of a God they don't believe in. They rattle off a litany descriptions and attributes that include an angry, wrathful God; a God who doesn't really care about or take part in life; a God who makes bad things happen to good people; etc., etc. and I have to retort by saying: Well, I don't believe in that God either.

I believe in and I believe a God who is not an abstract object. God is not watching us from a distance, as the song goes. God is eternal and infinite, but God is utterly imminent; God is right here and now, within and among everything and everyone. One might say that the universe is God's body, as if God even needs a body. God doesn't sit off somewhere on a cloud watching everything happen in the ongoing creation. God is making creation right here and now. For a long time the theo-logical community described God's role in creation as sometime long ago and far away God wound up creation like a clock and set it on a shelf and lets it do its thing. I believe that God is the clock. But even more so I believe that the nature of God, the character of God is best expressed by the words Loving and Gracious: the God Christ refers to and describes.

So Joshua asks the people "Choose this day whom you will serve." We should asks ourselves the same question over and over again as we wrestle with the forces, principalities and institutions that try to and in many ways do act as if they were (small g) gods unto themselves. Faith is not static: it has to keep growing, filling up the empty places in our lives and our world, so that we can experience and share the love and grace that God exists as and offers us and asks us to share among ourselves.

Some years back Bob Dylan wrote a song entitled, "You Gotta Serve Somebody." in which he sings of an incredible litany of professions, jobs, life-styles, attitudes pointing out the truth that no matter who you are you gotta serve somebody. Whether you're rich or poor, wealthy or broke, famous or unknown, powerful or powerless, big or small, white or black or brown or yellow or purple, you gotta serve somebody. The point is that serving somebody does not necessarily have to be oppressive. You have a family so you serve your family by taking care of them. Some might have jobs that they hate and find no meaning in, but they have to have an income so they have to serve the job; but they to have an income so they endure as best they can.

We all have situations in our lives where the service required of us can be oppressive, but in faith we can come around and know that the one we really are serving is God: not the God that we just believe in and just talk about as if God's in another room, but the God we know intimately and personally and, ultimately, the God we believe.

Knowing that we all gotta serve somebody, "Choose this day whom you will serve," and join in with all the faithful in saying "As for me and my house, we will serve the Lord; we will serve God."

Ever living, ever loving, ever present God, there are lots of choices we have to make in life, and a very important one, if not the most important choice is whether or not we believe in you, and, even more so whether or not we believe you. I know that sounds pretty simplistic, but you know as well as we do that you've got a lot of competition when it comes who and what we really put our faith in. Sometimes we feel like we're caught in a trap because there are forces in our lives that we cannot escape from.

The old prayer of confession says, "We have done that which we should not have done, and we have left undone that which we should have done." Sometimes this happens because of our own weakness or distraction, but sometimes this happens because we and pulled and pushed away from what you would have us do by forces we cannot contend with. Forgive us, our God, and help us always choose you and your ways of love and grace. Give us the strength to overcome those forces that would take us away from you.

When you offer yourself to us, you are offering ever present help and healing in all the ways we are in need of them. Help us open ourselves to the power of your presence in every situation we find ourselves in, both that we might be helped and healed, but also that we might truly be the helpers and healers you want us to be. Amen.

He/She/His/Hers/Him/Her: God

When I was back in Seminary, at Bangor Theological Seminary, in beautiful downtown Bangor, Maine, I had the honor of being a student of The Rev. Dr. Burton Throckmorton who was a world renowned authority on New Testament scripture, language and theology. It was during that time, back in the early seventies, that voices began to be heard in many theological circles questioning whether or not it was accurate or fair to envision God as being exclusively male; a man; a big, old man with long white flowing hair and beard, as in Michelangelo's Sistine Chapel. This question arose in concert with the emerging movement of more and more women going to seminary, being ordained and taking a much more active role in the leadership of the Church as well as in the larger theological arena. In some ways this was a very practical question: if God is exclusively a man where does that leave us as women? The deeper question was and is: is it biblically, theologically or historically accurate to assume that God actually is exclusively a man? This is the question that Dr. Throckmorton took head on, and in a nutshell the answer is no, it is not biblically, theologically or historically accurate to assume that God is exclusively a man. Again, I had the honor of being a student of Dr. Throckmorton as he worked through those questions and that process has had a profound effect on my life and ministry.

The biblical problem starts right at the beginning in the creation stories in the book of Genesis, and the problem is that there are two very different accounts of how God created human beings. In the first story it simply says, ". . . God created humankind in God's image, in the image of God, God created them; male and female God created them." The implication of this passage is very clear: if God created both male and female in God's own image, then God must be both male and female.

The second story is a little more complex and to simplify it let me say that God took some dust of the earth, mixed it with water, formed a man out of clay, blew breath into his nostrils and the man became a living being. Then God went on to create all the animals and plants, which the man named. Then God figured the man needed more than plants and animals for companionship, so God took a rib out of the man and created a woman. Then the man said, "This is at last bone of my bones and flesh of my flesh; this one shall be called Woman, for out of Man this one was taken." In Hebrew the actual words are, "... this one shall be called *Ishshah,* for out of *Ish* this one was taken." Contrary to many long standing interpretations of this story, there is no implication that the man was somehow superior to the woman because he was made first, the history of which I will get to shortly. The emphasis was on the fact that they were equal; both created by the same God which gives no indication that God was exclusively one or the other.

So where did this notion come from that God is exclusively a man? Part of the problem is quite simply a language issue. Neither Hebrew nor English nor most any other language has a neutral or inclusive pronoun. We have basically three ways to describe something or someone, besides their own name. These three pronouns are "he, she and it". We cannot escape the reality that the Hebrew culture was primarily patriarchal: men ruled, so it was rather natural, given the fact that they had to choose one pronoun that they would refer to God as "he". Therein lays the origin of the image of God being exclusively male: a man; he, him, his. But the question remains as to whether or not that is accurate or for that matter true.

If it was true, there certainly would be no references to God as anything remotely feminine or female in the Bible, and that simply is not true. There are many references to God as feminine, female or even more surprising Mother in the Bible. One of the most profound references to God as Mother is found in Isaiah 66: 10-13:

Another place we find many references to the feminine side of God is in the Wisdom literature, particularly in the books of the Song of Solomon, Wisdom of Solomon, and Proverbs where the main theme is that God is the source of wisdom, and even more so that wisdom is a characteristic of God; an attribute of God, and Wisdom as God's character and attribute is referred to exclusively as a woman: she, her, hers. This image of God as Wisdom is carried over into the New Testament as the Holy Spirit. So yes, believe it or not, the Holy Spirit originated as a feminine/female/woman characteristic/attribute of God. Kind of changes how we envision the Trinity. Father, Son and Holy Spirit were originally more like Father, Son and Mother.

So what happened? Where did all this feminine imagery of God disappear to? The Bible has been around for thousands of years and these representations of God as feminine have always been there. I never heard of them until I went seminary and the first time they were pointed out to me I was incredulous, and I've preached these words to many congregations and individuals therein who were equally incredulous. Why are they recently and currently coming to light?

Here we get into history and it's not all that pleasant. As I said before, the Hebrew culture was patriarchal: men ruled. Very few cultures in the world have always been anything but patriarchal, ours included. A few cultures have allowed women to participate in ruling a people primarily as Queens, but only in the absence of a King. The fact of the matter is that historically most cultures have been so patriarchal that the concept of a woman assuming a ruling position was utterly inconceivable. It was the ultimate "We've always done it this way." excuse. It wasn't really meant to be derogatory towards women it just was the way it was.

It wasn't until women started calling for some recognition and respect for themselves as other than wives and mothers that things turned derogatory. Just getting the right to vote was a major accomplishment. We won WW II and it was women who built the vast amounts of armament that made it possible and then were expected to go back to homemaking after it was all over. A door cracked open right then and there and it became inevitable that women would seek social, political and work force respect, as well as respect as Church leaders above and beyond Sunday school teachers. It was a long tough haul that we are still very much in the midst of.

The Protestant Church (most of denominations anyhow, ours included) was the first to really open up to women's leadership in ordination, but that wasn't by any means easy. I went to Bangor Theological Seminary primarily because my sister had had aspirations to go there years before, but between my father and the male Church leadership of the time, this simply was not acceptable. This was the early/mid sixties. When I started Seminary in 1971 there were only a handful of women in the school, and all but two of them were going for Christian Education degrees, not theo-logical degrees that led to ordination. One woman who graduated the year I started could not find an association that would ordain her.

Jump ahead a few years, 26 years to be exact, when my sister worked her way out of a job as a bank merger specialist, she went to Andover Newton and was ordained, has been serving congregations ever since. Today the vast majority of Protestant seminary students are women and in the rosters of many denominations (ours included) the majority of ordained ministers are women and is increasing. Things do change, however gradually or painfully.

A lot of men had (and some still have) lots of problems with women assuming authoritative roles in our society; positions that traditionally were held only by men. Part of this has to do with "That's the way it's always been.", but for millennia men had this inbred assumption that they were somehow superior to women; thus women were, and always had been inferior to men. When men were challenged as to why they felt they were superior to women, at the root of the reasons given, sometimes subtly and sometimes in your face blatantly was this: (ready?) men are superior to women because God is a man, and if you don't believe that just read the Bible. God the man created men and women, so the man must be more important than the woman. God the man created man first and women second, so it's obvious. The Bible doesn't talk about God being anything but a man. Even Paul in the New Testament puts women in their place.

So we come back to the original question: there are clear and definitive images of the feminine aspect of God throughout the Bible. It simply is not true that the Bible depicts God as being exclusively a male; a man, nor does it assign any exclusive authority to men over women. So where did these truths disappear to for so many centuries? They didn't; they were always there. They were ignored and they were suppressed by the Church male hierarchy because they compromised their exclusive patriarchal hold in the Church, as well as all forms of secular governments. They were brought back into the light of day by women who questioned if God is a man, then where does that leave us? They were brought back into the light of day by people like Dr. Throckmorton who had the courage to go looking for the truth and teach it to students like me.

I was indoctrinated with most of the male dominated attitudes that were predominant when I was a child. I resisted the changes that come with a new (actually ancient) image of God, but I came out the other end invigorated and liberated by being able to image God as both my Father and my Mother. My father is a very wise, caring and considerate man, but my mother taught me that I am loved and how to love. Both are attributes of God.

So how do we talk about God if God is not a male? We shouldn't call God he, him or his. It would be equally incorrect to call God she, her or hers. Back at the beginning I pointed out that this is a language problem; a pronoun problem and the only way around that problem is to not use a pronoun, use a name. Just refer to God as God. That's what I do. And when I read a translation or version of the Bible that hangs on to the male image, I see through it to the inclusiveness that God is all about.

One of the indoctrinations I endured was that men are stronger than women. When my then-wife gave birth to our first child, that notion went out the window forever. Men and women are equal in all aspects of what it means to be a human being. I know that because the Bible tells me so; God tells me so.

Open your hearts, minds and spirits to a truly inclusive image of God and you will find a new love and respect for everyone you share life with.

Creator God, parent God, ever living and loving God we envision you in many ways even if we cannot see you face to face as we do with other people. We have to use human imagery to describe you because that imagery is all we have to work with. Help us open our spiritual eyes, our faithful eyes and try engage an image of you as being so much more than we are, but equally real and present. Help us come to see you as our father and our mother for we know you truly are both at once. We use male imagery to describe you, but help us become comfortable and acceptable to using female imagery to describe you, for we know you truly are both at once.

As we come to recognize this equality in you, help us realize this equality in our personal and interpersonal lives. Help all fathers be the best fathers they can be. Help all mothers be the best mothers they can be, and help us all realize that as parents the two become one in the creation of our children, just as we become one in you.

There's a big storm coming our way, God. We would not be so arrogant that we would pray that it miss us and hit someone else. But we do pray that you will protect all in its path, minimize the damage and help people rebuild their lives when it has passed.

Amen.

Walking In the Dark

We were out of power for four days last week. It wasn't all that cold out, but we kept the wood stove going slowly just to take the damp chill out of the air. We have a gas range so we could cook and heat water. I had frozen a number of large coffee cans full of water and they did a good job of keeping our food cold. We have a couple of propane lanterns and a few good flashlights so we had enough light to function. On the second day power came on to most enclaves of houses around ours, but for some reason our enclave remained in the dark. Last year at this time we were out of power for eleven days and we survived quite nicely as I recall, but between the darkness, the roar of generators and the general inconvenience of it all, this outage bothered me more than usual, and I've been trying to figure out why.

I mean what's my problem after all? We endured just a few days of not having electricity while so many others were literally losing their homes and all their possessions, if not their lives. Entire communities were literally washed or burned away. It will take years to put it all back together again, and some communities will never be able to be rebuilt. We got off easy!

We walked around the neighborhood after dark a couple of times. In the houses with generators we could see the flickering lights of TVs. In the houses without generators we could see the flickering lights of lanterns or candles, and others were just plain dark. All of this made me aware of what was really bothering me, and that was the sad emptiness of it all. I was reminded of how when I was a kid, nobody in our neighborhood locked their doors or took their keys out their cars. There was no issue about going to someone's house to just hang around or to borrow something or ask for some help with a project or chore. We got together for holiday meals or just for the heck of it. Everybody knew everybody else's name. We walked around our neighborhood and I realized I knew the names of only two households, and there was little impetus to get to know more. I have friends who live in apartment complexes with dozens if not hundreds of other units, and they don't know the names of a single person in the whole place.

As our society has grown larger one would think that gaining and maintaining a sense of community would grow equivalently, but just the opposite has happened. People are ever more and more isolated from each other. People are ever more and more afraid of each other. The constant bombardment of bad news from the media just reinforces this paranoia. The American dream of owning one's own home has been reduced to owning one's own prison. So many people simply don't want a sense of community because they simply don't have any idea what a sense of community is. That's what was bothering me in the dark last week.

The Church is quite simply and ultimately profoundly a community; a community of believers who share in a common communion with God, Christ, each other and the whole of creation. Add to that the notion that this community extends both back in time to those who "have gone on" before us and those who will inherit our legacy in the future and we get a picture of what this communion of saints is all about. When we gather at this table go through our ritual of communion, we are doing two things: we are celebrating who we are as well as acknowledging what God and Christ are calling us to become.

The two who were walking down the road to Emmaus were walking in the dark: the darkness of having their hopes and dreams shattered at the death of their beloved Jesus. The stranger who was walking with them explained the situation but they didn't recognize that it was Jesus himself telling them the truth until he broke bread with them. That is the ritual we celebrate today: having our eyes opened and seeing the living Christ among us and within us. So look carefully and deeply into the eyes of the members of our communion of saints; our family and friends, the strangers on the street, and even in the mirror . . . you just see Jesus looking back at you.

Creator God, loving God, you create us to a family; we are indeed brothers and sisters of all humanity; all creation. You shower us with love and grace and we know how wonderful that can be, and that love and grace is what you offer us and ask us to share among all of us. But we build walls of indifference and fear between us. We classify each other in so many meaningless ways, instead of seeing each other and ourselves as your beloved children, equally cherished, equally blessed, and equally loved.

You call us into your Church to experience the community you call us to be. We exist and we live in communion with you, each other and all the peoples and creatures of our world. We symbolize this communion by sharing bread and the fruit of the vine and Jesus did with his followers, his disciples, his friends. Help us truly be his followers, disciples and friends. Help us truly be his living body and his life blood here in this church community, but also out there in what can be a cold, dark, scary world. Help us not be overcome by the darkness, but burst forth in loving light for the entire world to see.

Our God, there are so many people hurt and hurting around us; people suffering, people dying, people's lives being torn apart by giant storms and giant misunderstandings; giant wars, giant poverty, giant human-made pain. We ask you to step in God and stop the madness: fill us with your love and grace; make us whole and well again, and let us know; let us truly believe that whatever the world throws at us, in you, in Christ, we are more than conquerors in the power of your love and grace made real within and among us. Amen.

Giving Thanks—Letting Go—Letting God

When I was a little boy my parents taught me to always say "please" when asking for something and "thank you" when someone gave me something. On Thursday we will celebrate Thanksgiving which originated when the Pilgrims survived (most of them anyhow) the first year in the new world and they had a bountiful harvest to get them through the coming winter. Would it be that we had such straightforward needs to be met and thus to be thankful for. We don't have to worry about sheer survival like having enough food to eat during the winter. We don't have to worry about so many basic, human survival needs and I think it is fair to say that we often take them for granted.

I am acutely mindful of the fact that there are thousands of people in our own back yard who endured and are still enduring the wrath of Hurricane Sandy, and there are millions and millions of people around the world who live on the brink of death every day because they don't have food, water, shelter and sanctuary. They all are begging: "Please help us!", and we who have more than enough are called upon to answer their plea; to give them what they need so they can have something to say "Thank you." for.

It remains true that we of the first and second worlds are incredibly blessed. We don't have to say "Please God, can we have enough food and water and shelter to survive." so because we don't have to say "Please", we tend not to say "Thank you." And then there are the multitudes of things people don't really need to survive but they invest a great deal of time, energy and money making sure they have all these things, such as a the latest electronic gizmos, to the latest fashions, to the latest cars, and because people don't have to say "Please" to get them, they tend not to say "Thank you." when they do.

When I was a little boy Thanksgiving was also the beginning of the Christmas Season. I didn't know it at the time, but many people worked long hours on Thanksgiving Day itself to set up the wonderful, fantasy land, Christmas marquee on the front of the G. Fox building in downtown Hartford and on that Friday after Thanksgiving it was a tradition to go downtown at dusk and marvel at that spectacular sight. I wasn't aware at the time of the economic ramifications of Christmas (or Xmas), but today they all but overshadow the true meaning of Christmas with institutions like Black Friday; a term I personally abhor.

Thanksgiving was/is a time to give God thanks for all the basic human needs that God fulfills for us. Thanksgiving ushers in Advent when we relive the centuries of asking "Please God, give us a Messiah, an Emmanuel, a Savior, a Christ." On Christmas we celebrate that God has done so and with wide open hearts and minds we say "Thank you!"

Giving thanks; being thankful should not be a one-day-a-year event. Being thankful should be a mindset, a way of being that we celebrate every day. The fact that so many of us are so blessed makes it easy to forget that everything we are and everything we have originate as gifts from God. The fact is that the universe and all things that comprise the universe are gifts from God. The fact that we are here and now, alive and thriving is a gift from God. The fact that we have creativity, talents and abilities with which to provide for ourselves and each other is all a gift from God. We may have to *earn* a living, economically, but there is nothing we have to do or can do to *earn* existence and life. It's all; everything is a gift from God for which we should say "Thank you." with every breath we take.

Our annual Stewardship drive has begun, and being a good steward of all God has given and gives us is one good way of saying "Thank you." Every Church has to carry on it mission in part by being good stewards of their member's pledges and gifts of money, but a Church should not behave like a business in that they perceive themselves as producing some kind of product that they are trying to sell to the public. The Church is a portal in which the love and grace of God can be found, shared and celebrated. The Church is a vehicle by which the love and grace of God are indeed made real in people's lives. We don't, we can't earn the love and grace of God so we should not envision our stewardship drive and our gifts and pledges as somehow being earned. Sharing our bounty to make possible and enhance the mission of the Church should be as natural as breathing.

During the first couple of centuries that it existed, the Christian community was truly communal. No one earned anything, no one owned anything; everything was shared equally among all the members. It was not a question of giving something to the Church while keeping the rest for oneself. That sounds crazy in today's world, but at the heart of the matter is the truth that everything we are and all we have are the gifts of God which we are called upon to share with everybody else. In a true communal setting no one may own anything, but everybody has anything and everything they need. In recent history the Shakers embodied and enlivened that truth. Habitat for Humanity originated in a Christian community called Koinonia in Georgia in which everyone gives all their possessions to the community, which Millard and Linda Fuller joined and in doing so gave away their rather significant wealth, by which Habitat for Humanity was born.

I wouldn't, couldn't propose that our culture and society would ever embrace that ideal, but within the community of the Church it should be fully embraced if not actually lived out.

Each and every one of us has things we wonder about and things we worry about, and in today's world many of these things have something to do with money: whether or not we can afford something, whether it is our health care, our heating and electric bills, our mortgage or rent, or even the kind and amount of food we eat. Most everybody in this part of our society doesn't have the time or energy to worry about having what they *want,* because we are all preoccupied with making sure we can afford what we *need*. A big part of our society wastes an awful lot of time and energy worrying about whether or not they can afford everything they *want*, because they don't have to worry about having what they *need*. My parents survived the Great Depression and did their best to pass those values on to me. We always had what we needed, and when asking for something the request was always tempered with, "Is this something you want or something you need?"

Giving to the Church is one way of saying "Thank you." to God. For most of us the Church is the place and the community in which we first learned about God; in which our personal relationships with God were formed and nourished. Our stewardship of our own belongings includes sharing with the Church, and we are comforted by the truth that whether we have lots or little, we know that God knows what we need and does everything God can to make sure we have what we need. We hold that truth to be self evident whether we are talking about our own needs or the needs of the Church. All we are and all we have are the gifts of God for which we must be mindfully and openly thankful for at all times.

We can't always trust that our economy, our jobs, the stock market or the massive corporations that control our economy is going to give us a fair deal, but we can always trust that God is always going to give us a fair deal. When times get tough and we don't know if we can have everything we need, let go and let God. When it comes to giving to the Church let go and let God, and in all things be thankful.

Our Creator God, who gives us everything from the most essential realities of simply existing to the vast array of what it means to be a person; a human being: our lineages, our creativity, talents and abilities, our idiosyncrasies and all we hold in common, the miraculous workings of our bodies, hearts, minds and spirits, our families, friends, communities . . . for all this we bow before you and endeavor to say "Thank you!"

Remind us over and over and again and again that we never had to say "Please . . ." for what we now say "Thank you." You give all of this to us out of your totally unselfish, unconditional and unqualified love and grace. We do not have to earn it; we don't even have to ask for it: it's all there; it's all here for the taking, even though in reality it is not for the taking: it all is a given; given to us whether we know it or acknowledge it. What we have to do is become ever more mindful that all we are, individually and together; all we have individually and together, originate and will always remain your gifts for us. Help us truly set ourselves aside, and be filled with the spirit of "Thank you."

But oh, our God, there are so many ways that we all cry out "Please . . . help me." From the victims of natural tragedies, to the victims of oppression, injustice and war, from the sufferings of personal and collective infirmities and injuries, millions cry out "Please . . . help me . . . help us!" We know you are always with us . . . help us let go of our fears and let you be who and what you are. Help us let go of every other excuse we have and let you be our living, loving, ever gracious and ever present God. Thank you . . . Amen.

What Time Is It?

My routine for writing a sermon usually goes something like this. Sometimes, early in the week, I consult the lectionary scripture suggestions and if something rings a bell inside me I will ponder that idea through the week and on Friday I fire up my computer and put it on paper. Sometimes the lectionaries scriptures fall on deaf ears and I just sort of wait for an idea or a theme to pop into my head and off I go. What I have been doing these first few weeks I have been with you is to identify some rather general themes in our faith and life and use them as the basis for my sermon if only to give you some insight into who I am and what I'm all about. This past week I was all excited about anticipating preaching on the classic Advent themes, in part, at least, as an antidote to the Black Friday commercialized Xmas onslaught. So I thought and thought and pondered and pondered and on Friday I spewed forth an Advent sermon on Hope. I showed it to Debie for her perusal, as I usually do, and she said it was great . . . but, she also informed me, "This Sunday isn't the first Sunday in Advent." I responded "Whaddya mean? The Sunday after Thanksgiving is ALWAYS the first Sunday in Advent!" Well I consulted my UCC calendar and ate a piece of humble pie. She, as usual, was right. Thanksgiving is always the fourth Thursday in November, and if, as it was this year, the first Thursday in November is the first day of November, then another week gets added on at the end of November and the first Sunday in Advent goes with it. So I was challenged to do something that I very rarely do and really don't like to do and that was put that sermon on ice until next Sunday and, on Saturday morning, write something new. Doing that makes me feel like a short order cook. I like to have my sermons done on Friday so I have all day Saturday to ponder whether or not I made any major goofs or gained some new insight that I want to add on. On the brighter side of things I am all set for next Sunday, but all this left me pondering this question: "What time is it?", or, more to the point, "Who decides what time it is, or what day it is? Where do these calendars and lectionaries and traditions come from and why are we so beholden to them?"

The early Church didn't celebrate any holidays on an annual basis. They didn't remember or celebrate the day Jesus was born, or the day he died, or the day he was resurrected or the day he was baptized or the day he was transfigured or any other special events in his life that our Church traditions have cast in stone. The notion of establishing specific days of remembering and celebrating didn't come about until the Church was confronted with the pantheon of holidays celebrated by the pagan European Druids and the like who made real big deals about the Winter and Summer Solstices, the Spring and Fall equinoxes and Halloween. The Winter solstice represented the rebirth of the world as the sun stayed above the horizon longer each day. Well, let's celebrate Christ's birth in conjunction the Winter solstice . . . it all fits together. The Spring equinox represented the return of life to the world as the sun and warmth became strong enough to stir leaves and plants and baby rabbits and the like. Well, let's celebrate Christ's resurrection in conjunction with the Spring equinox . . . it all fits together. Remembering the dead on Halloween became the day we remember all the Saints . . . it all fits together. I am in no way trying to trivialize anything here. This is how our Church holidays came to be celebrated when they are.

Time is the most elusive thing in all of existence. We invented clocks and calendars to keep track of time; as a way of measuring time; as a way of measuring how long it has been since something happened (like when this sermon began) or how long it will be before something else happens (like when this sermon is over). We measure time in the past and in the future, but how can we or how do we deal with the reality of time which is ever and only and always this ever present moment we call "right now?" which is in constant movement, like a surfer riding a wave. The wave is time and the surfer is riding on that wave, moving through time and space. We and all of existence ride the ever moving wave of time which never wavers in its movement through time and space.

Our calendars give us the impression that time is cyclical: it goes round and round, repeating the same path year after year. Everything happens again and again at the same time of the year. This illusion is easily cracked by a birthday celebration: I was born on such and such a day according to our cyclical calendars, BUT, sixty something years have passed since that day actually happened. Obviously, as Joni Mitchell so eloquently sings:

> And the seasons they go 'round and 'round
> And the painted ponies go up and down
> We're captive on the carousel of time
> We can't return we can only look behind
> From where we came
> And go round and round and round
> In the circle game

Our seasons certainly do seem to be cyclical in nature, but in actuality they are not. November 25, 2012 is in no way the same as November 25, 2011 was, nor as 2013 will be. We're not the same people we were a year ago or will be a year from now. As the hymn "O God, Our Help in Ages Past" sings, according to the New Century Hymnal: "Time, like and ever rolling stream, soon bears us all away, we fly forgotten, as a dream fades at the opening day." I appreciate the poetic nuances of that verse, but I don't necessarily agree with them. Time does bear us along our ways, but we are not forgotten like a dream. All of my ancestors live on in me and I and we all will live on in all my offspring. Time may appear to be cyclical like a wheel, but it's more like a wheel rolling down a road. It's constantly moving and will never be in the same place it once was or will be. Time doesn't go 'round and 'round or up and down: time moves in an unwavering straight line into the future.

The writer of Ecclesiastes points out very poetically that God has a different perspective on time than we do. I like to try to imagine that God is somehow outside of time and looks on time as a continuum that only God can see from beginning to end, and knows the infinity and eternity of the past and future all at once. We can't really grasp that kind of concept because we are stuck in space, riding along on time. Though we can remember the past (as best our memories can allow this), and we can endeavor to imagine the future, all we can ever know for certain is what is happening right now in this ever present moment we call right now, and even our perceptions of that can be questionable at times as we each and all have slightly or profoundly different perspectives on what is happen right now.

There was a fascinating program on NPR's Science Friday a couple weeks ago in which some psychologists and neurologists were discussing how our perceptions of time differ according to the situation we're in at the time and even in our own personalities. We like to say that time flies when we're having fun and time slows to a crawl when we're bored out of our minds. People talk about time standing still when they are in a crisis situation, and in what seems to be just an instant their whole life flashes before them in their minds. The speed of time doesn't change but our perception of time certainly does. When I was little and I was bored waiting for something like Christmas or my birthday my mother would always say something to the effect, "Be patient, don't push it, time goes faster and faster the older you get and one day a whole year will just flash by." She was certainly right. Don't just seize the day, savor the day. This is the day, the hour, the ever present moment that God has made for us. Rejoice and be glad in it.

So even if today isn't the first Sunday in Advent, it is still the day God has made for us and we are the people God has made this day for. Let us all give thanks for that.

Creator God, constantly creating, constantly making all things new, we stand in awe of you. Sometimes time seems to fly by, sometimes is just drags along and sometimes we wish we could slow it down, and we thank you for the comfort of knowing you are with us at all times and in all the situations we find ourselves in. You know us from before our beginnings and further into the future than we can imagine.

Help us savor each and every day as your gift to us, your children who you love so. Help us ride the waves of time using our talents and abilities; our creativity, wisely, not just for our benefit but for the benefit of all we share time and space with; all we share life with. You call us to love each other as you love us. Help be mindful of that truth in all the times, places and situations we find ourselves in, taking the time to reach out to one another in your love.

There are times, God, when we find ourselves wondering or worrying, happy or sad, whole or broken, alone and lonely, beset with illness, enduring injuries to our bodies, minds, hearts and spirit. Help us feel your loving presence as you guide and assure us, as you help and heal us, as you hold our hands and walk with us down the paths of time.

Help take the time to open ourselves to your presence in our ever present here and now; to share freely our wonders and worries, our needs and our wants; the needs and wants of other. Amen.

What Are We Waiting For? Hope!

It's no coincidence that the words Invent and Advent sound so similar. To invent something means a person is making something new. Advent means that we are waiting for something new; we are anticipating something new. There is air of mystery surrounding the word Advent because, as it is in an ad-venture, we know something is going to happen, but we're not quite sure what. Advent is a time of reflecting on what we hope will happen. Advent is a time of remembering what it was like before Christ came, when all hearts were yearning for God to do something; to make something special happen; to make a personal appearance in our lives and in our world; to e-man-uel: to be with us and somehow straighten out our crazy, mixed up and messed up world and our crazy, mixed up and messed up lives. But Advent is not only a time of remembering what it was like before Christ came. Advent is a time of acknowledging, reflecting and confessing all the ways that Christ has not yet come into our world and into our lives.

There are four main themes in our traditional observance of Advent and they are Hope, Peace, Love and Joy, and it's no coincidence that the first one is Hope, because Hope is what Advent is all about, and as Paul tells the Hebrews, Faith is what Hope is all about. "Now faith is the assurance of things hoped for, for the conviction of things not seen . . . By faith we understand that the worlds were prepared by the word of God, so that what is seen was made from things that are not visible."

There is a good dose of imagination that comes with Hope. What we hope for is often something we can only imagine. Imagine a world in which there are no wars, no strife, no oppression, and no injustice. Imagine a world in which all people live whole, healthy and happy lives with plenty to eat and drink and solid and secure shelter from the elements. Imagine a world in which all people enliven the truth that we actually all are brothers and sisters, mothers and fathers to each other, because we know we each and all are indeed the children of our living, loving God. Imagine peace, imagine plenty, and imagine love between, within and among all people. As hard as it can be to imagine all these things in a word that is in so many ways devoid of them, we must imagine all these things because they are what our hope and our faith are all about. If our faith does not include the hope that all these good things will come about, because God says so, then what are we doing here? If we don't have that hope, if we don't have that faith, then we might as well join the teeming masses at the mall and forget what Christmas is all about.

We hope for all these things; we believe that all these good things will come to be, because God says so. Even at a purely humanistic level all people want to live good, whole, healthy and happy lives; that's what being a human being is all about. Aside from a relatively few, but very vocal and violent fundamentalist, militant radicals in many religions and institutions, who turn the word of God inside out and upside down proclaiming that God only wants a certain, select minority to live good, whole, healthy and happy lives, the word of God in many languages and many traditions says quite clearly that God knows what we need to live good, whole, healthy and happy lives and promises, GOD PROMISES that the day will come when all people will live good, whole, healthy and happy lives. Our faith assures us that this is true. Our faith is our hope, and having that hope should, must affect the way we live our lives. If we have faith, if we believe that all these things are going to come about we have to accept the responsibility that comes with this faith and this hope, which is to say we have to help make them happen.

Hope is as necessary for human survival as is breathing. The need for hope grows within us as we grow up from a totally dependent infant whose every need is quickly met, into adolescence where we start to be confronted by the choices and uncertainties of life, into adulthood where we begin to get smacked with the reality that life really is a one way street; where choices and circumstances deeply affect the relativity of our sense of well being. Sometimes things go our way and sometimes they don't. When confronted with a crisis we call upon our hope to get through it. When called upon to make decisions that affect our lives and others lives, we hope to make the right choice. When faced with the finitude of life we call upon our hope to avoid if not face up to the end. Our faith is our hope based on God's promises.

Hope is relative to the existential circumstances that we face in a given time and place. A beggar on the street hopes for a warm shelter and a decent meal. A person in a war zone hopes to make it through the day alive. A victim of persecution hopes to one day be liberated. An injured person or a person who is facing a serious illness hopes to be healed and cured. A person facing a painful death hopes to get it over with. Hope comes in many forms as a response to real needs and there is nothing worse that can happen in any person's life than to lose all hope, but that has happened and happens altogether too often.

We may hope to get the raise and promotion we want. We may hope to get a certain Christmas present. Again the difference between real needs and ambiguous wants needs to be clarified here. In my family we rarely ask "What do you want for Christmas?" If someone asks me that question I simply reply "Surprise me.", inviting them to delve into their knowledge of me and/or their relationship with me to perceive what I might need or want. The original Christmas present was a total surprise. People hoped that God would do all sorts of things to make God's presence and power known; to usher in an area to be called "The Kingdom of God." Some hoped for a mighty warrior or king who would vanquish all of our foes and enemies and establish an everlasting peaceful and prosperous rule (Some people still hope for that, if not expect it). Some hoped for some kind a supernatural, cosmic event, if not calamity, that would eliminate all oppressors and persecutors and all bad people in general, allowing all the good, chosen people to inherit the earth and live in peace and plenty forever. (Some Christians still hope for that, if not expect it.) Neither is what we got. What we got was a baby born in a manger to a poor unmarried couple who grew up into a teacher and healer who would change the course of human history forever, not by making the Kingdom of God happen instantaneously, but by inviting us to make it happen ourselves, and teaching us and assuring us that we can BECAUSE GOD SAYS SO! We hope for the coming of the Kingdom of God not because we're waiting for God to do it all for us, but because God assures us that we, with God's guidance and help, CAN DO IT!

Not everybody believes that the Christ has come. Emmanuel, which literally means "God is with us", the Lamb of God, the Rose of Sharon, the Prince of Peace, the Son of David, the Son of Man, the first-born, full—fledged Child of Humanity, the Son of God; call him by any name you wish: to those who believe, the Chosen One, the Anointed One, the Christ has come and is still with us. Don't waste your time waiting for Jesus to come back again because he's already come back. That's what the resurrection is all about.

The hope that God assures us of is not just that God is almighty and all powerful and eternal and infinite and imminent and living and loving and omniscient and omnipresent etc. etc. ad infinitum. We already know that. The hope that God gives us is again not that God is going to do it all for us, but that we already have within our own beings all that it takes to bring about the goodness, the wholeness, the wellness, the happiness that we all yearn for. God gives us hope, not only hope in God, but hope in ourselves; hope in each other; hope in humanity; hope in all of God's children. But, in the end, it is up to each and every one of us to put the love and grace of God that we find in Christ to work in our lives bringing about all we yearn for, all we hope for. If we take that simple, single, small step God will always be Emmanuel; God will always be with us, within us and among us helping to the point of promising that together with God, we can bring about the Kingdom of God right here on earth.

God, please grant us hope. In the face of darkness may there be light. In the face of doubt may there be faith. In the faith of fear may there be courage. In the face of death may there be life. In the face of despair let there be hope.

Even though we go through the same cycle year after year, knowing that Christ has come, we need to be reminded that there are many places in our lives and in our world where Christ has not yet come; where we tend to still leave him in the manger and not let him into our homes, our lives and our hearts. Christ came for all people everywhere: not just one race, not just one nation, not just one community of people who share the same traditions, not just one person. In the face of the despair of watching, if not experiencing the struggles and strife, the war and terror, the blatant absence of peace within and among nations and religions and peoples and persons; in the face of such despair grant us hope, fill us with hope and enable and empower us to be living witnesses to your promises, your love and grace, that by our example others might be led to join in our hope and make that hope real and fulfilled for everybody.

There are places deep in our hearts and minds where we struggle with despair in our own worries about ourselves and our relationships. There are places where our bodies fail us, our minds deceive us and we need to know the hope that you are always with us, offering your guidance and healing in all the ways we need to be healed and made whole.

'Tis the season of silence in which we anticipate your Advent into our world and lives. Help us listen carefully to this wondrous silence and hear your now whispered promises explode in the reality we call life. Amen

PEACE

One of my favorite quotes from the Christian author Fred Buechner is this:

"Peace has come to mean (a) time when there aren't any wars, or even when there aren't any major wars. Beggars can't be choosers; we'd most of us settle for that. But in Hebrew peace, shalom, means fullness, means having everything you need to be wholly and happily yourself.

"One of the titles by which Jesus is known is Prince of Peace, and he used the word himself in what seem at first glance to be two radically contradictory utterances. On one occasion he said to the disciples, "Do not think that I have come to bring peace on earth; I have not come to bring peace, but a sword." And later on, the last time they ate together, he said to them, "Peace I leave with you; my peace I give to you."

"The contradiction is resolved when you realize that for Jesus peace seems to have meant not the absence of struggle but the presence of love."

It's a whole lot easier to talk about the absence of peace; the presence of struggle, strife, conflict and war, than it is to talk about the presence of peace because, at least according to nearly all news sources, there's a whole lot more to talk about in war than in peace. The world is chock full of ongoing and long standing conflicts and wars, some with unimaginably horrific consequences for the opposing armies, but even more so by the innocent populations caught in the cross fire or used as examples in horrible acts of terrorism. Used to be that when two or more peoples went to war with each other each side put on a definitive uniform and they set up defined battle lines and at daylight they went at each other with whatever weapons they had at hand and at dusk they went back to their camps, buried their dead, tended their wounded, ate supper, had a bit to drink and went to bed, and went through the same drill the next day until one side surrendered or ran away. I once watched a revolutionary war reenactment and I couldn't believe how the soldiers lined up, shoulder to shoulder, about fifty feet apart and at point blank ranger fired their guns at each other. Then they all had to stop and reload and then they went at it again. As the technology of war and weapons evolved over time, war became much less personal; less and less face to face, until today a person can fire a weapon and obliterate an entire town, city or even an individual person half way around the world with deadly and devastating accuracy. The various terrorist groups around the world keep it much more personal with non-descript suicide bombers who most often target civilians and soldiers alike, often including their own people, to terrorize the population into submitting to their particular understanding of their particular religious sect or political ideology. The causes and effects remain the same in all cases. For whatever reasons, one side wants to conquer or just destroy the other side, which becomes retaliatory, and you've got a war in which countless people suffer and die both on the battlefield and as "collateral damage." The more advanced the weaponry, the more people suffer and die

Wars don't start on a battlefield or in a general's office or in government chambers. Many emerge from long histories. The Nazi's assumption that the Germans were the superior race originated in tribal times, centuries before the 1930s. Fueled by perverted interpretations of Darwin's theories about the origins of the species and the survival of the fittest gave them permission to make such a claim and make their plans for the conquest of Europe, if not the whole world. Animosity towards and hatred of the Jews had been around for centuries, ever since they had been kicked out of Israel by first the Romans and later the Christians. The Nazi's holocaust was not the first attempt to eradicate the Jews from at least Europe if not the whole planet, and that threat is still there in the names of Hazbala and Iran.

The wars going on in the Middle East find their origins in ancient tribal feuds which are justified by a very perverted interpretation of Islam, in which God not only approves of but commands the elimination of all non Islamists, including Islamists in various "other" Islamic sects. I do not understand how people can interpret a theology in which the Creator of all that is would wish for, let alone order the suffering and death of people; it does not compute. I understand what happens, but I don't understand how it happens or why it happens. I've said it before and I'll keep on saying it: (to put it nicely) I am deeply suspicious of the validity of any religion that promotes prejudice, intolerance, oppression of or violence against any people. "Them's fighting words!" . . . well that's my point exactly.

And that's enough about the presence of war, so let's move on to the potential for the presence of peace.

Reasons, ideologies even religions that create and promote war do not come into being in a vacuum. People invent them; people create them; people nourish them and propagate them. Wars and rumors of wars find their origins in human beings; in their hearts and minds, spirits and bodies, and if we ever are going to achieve true peace it will begin by changing people's hearts. If we are ever going to usher in an age in which there is the true presence of love and, as Buechner says, "(everybody) *having everything you need to be wholly and happily yourself.*", it will begin with people changing their hearts, or maybe better said, by people allowing their hearts to be changed. That's what Jesus' teachings are all about. He didn't come proclaiming a new theology. He didn't come to change our minds. He didn't come to create a new religion, or set up a new hierarchical, patriarchal structure of doctrines and dogmas that provide a framework which can support the assumption that we're right and everybody else is wrong. He came to change people's hearts: to instill empathy, compassion, acceptance, understanding; the rudiments of love in people's hearts which are the rudiments, the seeds of peace. He taught by example; by showing us how much God loves us; by showing us what true miracles can happen when people actually do love one another even as we are loved by God. You can't love somebody with your mind. You can only love somebody with your whole being. God loves our whole beings with God's whole being, and we won't find true peace until we do the same to ourselves and each other.

Even in the midst of the madness of maintaining and promoting cultural, social, political and religious intolerance against and oppression of other people, the perpetrators still want to be whole and happy themselves; they want to be loved. How they can want to or expect to be whole and happy and loved themselves while at the same time making others people's lives miserable, if not destroying them, is beyond me . . . but there are a lot of things about being human that are beyond me. And, if it wasn't for the love of God made known in Jesus Christ, I'd probably just give up on humanity and withdraw into my own selfishness, as many people of many persuasions, religions and walks of life do.

Before a person becomes a political or social ideolog or a religious zealot, they are first and foremost a person that simply wants to be whole, happy, healthy and loved. That's what being a human being is all about. In a psychological nutshell, if a person is not at peace within and with themselves, they will take it out on others by denying them their peace. Next week I'll be talking about love (expect a really long sermon), but for now I want to put forth the truth that even as a person cannot love someone else if they don't love themselves, it is equally difficult if not impossible for people to be at peace with each other if they are not at peace within and with themselves. That kind of peace is what Jesus is talking about when he says, "Peace I leave with you; my peace I give to you. I do not give you (peace) as the world gives you (peace)." Christ gives us the true peace of knowing we are loved beyond measure by our God who only wants and intends for us all to be whole, happy and healthy no matter what peacelessness we might encounter and endure in our lives. That is what the Good News is all about.

Knowing we are loved beyond measure by our Creator; the Creator of everything and everyone, is the seed that becomes knowing true peace within and with ourselves, and that peace is the source from which true peace among ourselves can come into being. Its one thing to know we are loved and be at peace within and with ourselves and it's quite another to spread that peace with and among all the people we share life with, but the two do go hand in hand. We can only find peace by making peace happen.

Our God, our Creator, our Father, our Mother, our brother and sister, you know full well all the times and places, the situations and circumstances, in which our lives and our communities and our nations and our whole world knows and experiences anything but peace; and in the absence of peace, we know only uncertainty, anxiety, worry, fear, despair, trauma, terror and death. And in the face of that darkness you offer us light. In the face of that uncertainty, anxiety, worry, fear and despair you offer us Hope. In the face of that terrible peacelessness you offer us Peace, and by your living example in Jesus the Christ, you show us the way to not only know peace, but to make peace, within us and among us.

Our God, please help us face up to the sources of peacelessness in our hearts, our minds, our spirits, our bodies, our communities, our nations and our world, because the source of our peacelessness is the absence of love. Help us breed within and among ourselves the seeds of peace: compassion, empathy, understanding, tolerance and the willingness to let go and let be; to let go and let you; to let go and let God work within, among and through our hearts and minds and spirits to come to realize we all are your beloved children, and as such each and every one of us deserves and has reason to expect that we will be loved and we will love each other as deeply truly and faithfully as you love us. Amen

LOVE

For the better part of the last century, scientists have been trying to identify a single mathematical formula that would explain everything about everything; how matter and energy and time and space came into being and how it all continues to interact as all of existence moves through time, from the past, through the present and into the future. Einstein's Theory of Relativity sets the stage for the assumption that such a Unifying Principle, in theory, might exist. Quantum mechanics point in the same direction. But not being a scientist and not pretending to know what I just said actually means, I look from a different perspective on the proposition that there is one, single, unifying principle and truth that explains how every has come to be; where it all came from and where it's all going, and that one single (to use a very bold word:) **TRUTH** is **Love**.

Scientists try to explain how everything works; how everything came to be what it is and where it's all going in the future. These are mostly good, creative and necessary endeavors, and our lives would be pretty much meaningless and worthless without them. I have no quarrel with science and I see no reason for there to be conflicts between science and religion as long as each maintains its own unique perspective. Science endeavors to explain **HOW** things are what they are, and religion, at least our own brand of Christianity, endeavors to explain **WHY** things are as they are. The classic debate over whether God created everything in six days, or in evolutionary process that has been going on for billions of years is a good case in point. In my opinion, science trumps the Biblical writers in sheer knowledge of historical fact, but science has no reason or expectation to even try to explain **WHY** things are as they are. Our answer to that question, in the truth of our faith, is quite simply and profoundly **Love.**

From the perspective of our faith, understanding how things came to be is not nearly as important as understanding, in our faith, why things came to be. Why did/does God bring creation into being?

God's single, unifying principle or reason is that God loves Creation and everything in and about it. God loves Creation into being. Love is why God does this. God's primary motivation in all things is Love. God does not reason things into being, though God creates reason as part of Creation. God does not emit love as an emotion, though God creates emotions as part of Creation. God is anything but indifferent to or aloof from Creation, as a carpenter might create a piece of furniture and set it aside from one's self when it's done. No, God is imminently and intimately involved in every aspect and moment of Creation. There is nothing that exists that is not imminently and intimately involved with God by God continually loving everything into being.

One poet put forth an image that I like to play with sometimes and that is that the universe, the Cosmos is God's body, but there some limits to that image. The word Pantheism has been around a long time, and Pantheism means, essentially that God **IS** everything. A relatively new word, Panentheism means that God is not everything, but God is **IN** everything. All three images attempt to put forth the awareness that God is not just a big, old man sitting on a throne up in heaven someplace watching us from a distance. God is not in one place and time not in another place and time. God is everywhere and every when all at the same time, and why God is everywhere and every when all at once is that God loves everywhere and every when always, infinitely and eternally.

In Psalm 139 the psalmist asks "Where can I go from your Spirit? Or where can I flee from your presence?" At length, the answer is nowhere or no when or no way. Now if you're afraid of God that's a rather scary notion and can lead to problems with guilt and paranoia. But, if you know that the infinite and eternal presence of God is motivated by God's infinite and eternal love, that's mighty good news.

What do we experience when all the plants and animals of the earth come to life in the Spring and sprout and bloom and birth and multiply in prolific abundance? We are experiencing the infinite and eternal love of God. What do we experience as plants bear fruit during the Summer, ripening both as food for other living things and seeds for the next generation? We are experiencing the infinite and eternal love of God. What do we experience as we watch vegetation seem to die, but we know they are actually just hunkering down for another cold Winter getting prepared for next Spring? We are experiencing the infinite and eternal love of God. When we experience the wonder of loving and being loved by spouses, family and friends; when we experience something beautiful like a sunset or sunrise; something beautiful created by other people as music and the other arts; when we experience any and all good things we are experiencing the infinite and eternal love of God, and soaking up that love in the good times make the dark, dreary, empty and lonely times bearable because we know the love of God is always and always will be with us, within us and among us. That's what the Good News is all about.

A person cannot reason one's way into love. Love can sometimes be very unreasonable, even irrational, and to a point that's OK. Though love is often very emotional, both sometimes happy and ecstatic as well as sometimes seemingly infinitely painful, love is much more than a collection of emotions. Love has its own collection of physical realities, but love is much more than physical. Love has its own collection of spiritual realities. The bond that people find in love often has very real spiritual dimensions. So, yes, love involves reason, emotion, the body, spirituality; love involves the mind, the heart, the body and spirit all at once. In a nutshell, love is a very wholistic experience, and, as far as we know, it is pretty much a uniquely human wholistic experience, though we all have observed the bonds of affection and trust that can develop between various animals, and between people and animals. If the love of God is indeed with, within and among all of God's Creations, then certainly all God's critters can experience it in its own way.

It is very difficult to define love because it is such a conglomeration of experiences and relationships. One cannot teach a person what love is. One can only show a person what love is by loving them and drawing love out of them; by inspiring them to experience their own love by giving love back in return; by sharing their love in relationships. So when God wanted to show us human critters the infinite and eternal depths and breadths of God's love for each and every one of us, what would the most practical way to do this? It would be for God to come to us in person, as a person and love us in person, which is, in my opinion exactly what happened on the original Christmas, and through fog of the hustle, bustle and mania of commercialized Christmas, that truth remains as real and true as it was a couple of thousand years ago.

I like to think of the experience of God's love as a kind of awakening. Though we are immersed in and surrounded by God's infinite and eternal love, we may often find ourselves unaware of it, and waking up to it can be a life changing experience. My first, what I would call, spiritual awakening was when I was a young boy watching the sky after a thunderstorm. The power of the wind and the rain and the lightning and thunder overwhelmed me, and then as the clouds moved on and the sun shone through the openings in the clouds and the sound of the thunder moved off in the distance I was simply filled with the power of it all, and I found myself filled with the sense of knowing to the bottom of my being that God simply is. Like Elijah expecting but failing to find the presence of God in a violent wind storm, a strong earthquake and an all consuming fire, he found God in the still, small voice that followed. God's love is very subtle, but utterly profound and once one experiences it, it can and will never be forgotten or ignored again.

It's a real truth that it is very difficult if not impossible to love someone else if you do not or cannot love yourself. People who don't experience being loved and living in a loving relationship simply don't know what love it in the personal, practical, existential reality that love is. For me, the most meaningful aspect of God's love in my life, is knowing, throughout my whole being, that God loves me and everybody else just the way we are, unconditionally, no matter what baggage we carry from the past, or how much time we've spent on the highways of regret. Knowing that God loves and expresses that infinite and eternal love in and through all of creation tells us how much we are loved and can inspire us to look at every other person in a new light: God loves each and every one of you as much as God loves me, and therein lie the seeds of love that will one day sprout, blossom and bear the fruit of true love; God's love, in and among all people.

And even in the midst of the darkness, the madness, the horror, the insanity, the disbelief, the tragedy of these days, the one rock, the one truth, the one reality we can hold on to for dear life is the love of God. God loves and will always love those children and those adults. God loves those parents, their friends, all their relatives, the first responders, the police, the agents; God loves all who are involved in the madness of trying and failing to make sense of this madness; and in the end: after the wind, after the earthquake, after the fire . . . there is only the still, small voice of God whispering, saying, screaming above the din of confusion and despair . . . I love you . . . I cannot change what has happened . . . but I am infinitely and eternally with you, among you and within you . . . because I love you.

At Christmas God is simply telling us, in what becomes a new way every day: "I Love You!"

Our God, it is an essential and intimate part of our faith to know you love us . . . we know it is true, it is real, it is the source of life itself . . . we know you invite us, you ask us, you call us to revel in the wonders of your love and make them real within us and among us so that we can share in and enliven your love within and among us all . . .

These days it is particularly difficult to know that or do that in light of the fact that one of your children, even your beloved child, could do what he did in that school in Newtown to others of your beloved children . . . it doesn't make any sense, it is crazy, it is insane, it is meaningless and purposeless, it's nuts . . . and the darkness threatens to overwhelm us . . .

We need to hear from you either in a loud and thunderous wind storm, earthquake or fire . . . or in a still small voice . . . we need to hear from you . . . why you allow these things to happen, and what you can and will do for all of us in its aftermath.

Remind us that you are indeed the lord of life as well as death . . . that even in the darkness you promise us light . . . even in the midst of doubt and despair, you offer us hope . . . even in the midst of anything but peace, you offer us peace . . . even in the midst of anything but love, you are still loving us, calling us to love one another even as you love us.

Of our God, we hurt for those who have been hurt; for those who have lost everything: their most beloved . . . help us hold on tight to all we are loved by and love for . . . knowing that in the darkness you are still with us, still loving us and calling us to all we can to love each other even as you love us. Amen.

Christ Is Come!

Ebenezer had a choice
He could continue to relive his Christmas past that made him a Scrooge
He could succumb to his Christmas future with its empty nothingness
Or he could change his Christmas present and allow Christ to be born in himself

Every Christmas we should celebrate all three
Yes, Christ DID come
Christ HAS come
Christ WAS born
But, Yes, Christ IS come
Christ IS born
But, Yes, Christ WILL come
Christ WILL be born

Christmas is not a once upon a time event
Christmas is not a once in history event
Christmas is not a once in a lifetime event
Christmas is the ever present possibility
That God promises will happen
Again and again and again and again . . .
Every time and in every way it is needed,
Which is pretty much always and in all ways

Christmas is all about a child being born
Christmas is all about God being born
In us within us and among us
2000 or so years ago
This morning, tomorrow morning, Christmas morning
Every morning

God lights the lights that overcome the darkness
God decorates our world like a Christmas tree
God gives us hope
God gives us peace
God gives us love
God gives us joy
God gives us life
God gives us God's own self
Each and every day in every way we can need them
So that each and every day we can share them with each other
And make everyday Christmas for everyone.

So for me, that's what Christmas is all about
'Nuff said . . . let's all say "Merry Christmas!"
Let's all say ". . . and to all a good night!"

We welcome you, our Lord and our God with open arms, open minds, open eyes and open hearts. You have come to us as one of us and we thank you by coming to you; by letting you into our lives, that we might truly find and live into and live out the hope, the peace, the love and the joy that this night is all about.

Maybe we thought we wanted or expected a mighty warrior, a perfect politician, a shrewd negotiator, someone whose authority was so blatantly obvious that no one could question their intentions. That's not what we got . . . that's not what you gave us . . . that's not how you presented yourself to us. You came as one of us: born as we are born . . . a child like we once were or maybe still are . . . a living, breathing, learning, growing human being just like us . . . so you could show us in person how much you love us and how good it truly is when we learn to love one another. Yet your wonder, your strength, your might, your authority is not to be found in human conditions, but in the simple humility of a love given to an offered by a newborn child.

Our God, there are so many places in our lives and in our world that await your birth, your presence and your love . . . help we who tonight celebrate your birth within and among us be living witnesses of and to all the wonders of your love. Amen.

"... FROM THE EAST ..."

An Epiphany is a moment of striking realization; a sudden and unexpected wake—up call; an "oh ho!" moment; a moment in time when one realizes that something brand new has happened or is happening. In our tradition the epiphany we celebrate today is the realization that Jesus is the Christ; Jesus is God made flesh and dwelling among us, and Matthew uses the wonderful little story of the Magi to usher in our Epiphany.

The pressing question that pops up with this wonderful little story is who were these Magi people? Straight from the Greek comes the word Magi, but we sometimes call them the three Kings or the three Wise Men. Actually, the only reason we assume that there were three of them was because they presented three gifts. Matthew only says Magi came. How many doesn't matter as much as who they were. One serious clue as to who they were can be found in other ways that we have come to use the word Magi, and, hold on to your socks, we commonly use the word Magi in two ways: in magic and magician.

Historically the Magi, which is plural for Magus, were priests of the Zoroastrian religions found in the East: in Persia and Medes at the time of Christ. At that time and in that religion there was no separation between Church and State. The religious leaders; the priests, were the rulers and the leaders of the whole society. They weren't kings in the sense that an individual was the supreme ruler. The Magi were a caste, a class of people, all priests, who maintained, conducted and oversaw the religious life of the people. They were very highly regarded and respected as authorities over every aspect of life.

The Zoroastrian religion is believed to have originated well before the 6th century BC in the Mesopotamian valley, which is presently centered in the Iraq and Iran area, which is the ancient homeland of just about every culture and religion on earth. As our ancient ancestors migrated north out of Africa the Mesopotamian valley became a common settlement area and later a hub from which peoples migrated north, east and west. The origins of the Zoroastrian religion are lost in time but many scholars believe that its original forms are probably the origins of just about every religion on earth. Quite simply put, the Zoroastrians believe that life and all existence is caught up in a duality of good versus evil, light versus dark, and the practice of the religion is to emphasize and realize the goodness and counter, if not overcome the badness. This simple duality or dichotomy is common, in many various forms, to all religions. So it is appropriate to trace the influence of Zoroastrianism to everybody from the Druids to the north, the Egyptians to the west, the Hindus and Buddhists to the East and every variation in between, including the Jews, the Muslims, and, you got it, we Christians.

The Zoroastrians practiced astrology which is very common among many religions, but what is most remarkable about the appearance of the Magi in Bethlehem is not how they got there, by following a star, but that they were there at all. At the time they were most certainly the largest religion on earth, but, in the Hebrew tradition, they were witches, sorcerers, enchanters, shaman, possessors of demonic powers; all pagan heretics who were banned from Jewish faith and society and were to be openly and brutally persecuted if caught in action. What is ironic is that when Joseph presented himself to Pharaoh as one who could accurately interpret dreams, he was presenting himself as a Magus, and later on Saul's fatal flaw was that he consulted a witch of Endor to divinize the outcome of his battle with the Philistines, which he lost. Actually, the work of the Magi's divinations is not all that different from the works of the prophets. The biggest difference, and the reason that the Hebrews so vehemently outcast and persecuted the Zoroastrians, was that, according to the Hebrews, the prophets got their information directly from God; from Yahweh, whereas the Magi got their information from astrology, sorcery, false gods and other non-Hebrew shamanic sources.

Matthew was rather brave and bold to include this little story about Magi following a star to come and worship the new born Christ; the King of the Jews. Lucky for them the Romans were actually very tolerant of various "other" religions and their presence probably protected the Magi from the hands of the Jews. It's interesting to note that Herod, upon hearing the Magi's divinations about Jesus, turned to the Jewish authorities to verify if they were true even though the vast majority of the Jews did not believe they were true, nor did they ever recognize Jesus as the Christ; the Messiah.

At the heart, the core, the bedrock bottom line assertion and presentation of this story is that people of other radically different religions with radically different approaches to their faith and the practices of their faith could, did and do recognize Jesus as the Christ; the Messiah. It's a little difficult to get our heads wrapped around how radically profound that assertion really is. We are so steeped in Western European culture and tradition, especially when it comes to our particular brands of our Christian faith, that it is very difficult to imagine being a Christian without being a Western European and/or, in our case, and American. During the age of colonization, better known as the age of slavery, the assertion was that upon encountering a native population the goal of these righteous "Christians" was to convert the population to Christianity which actually meant more so to convert them to Western European culture.

In 1452 Pope Nicholas V issued this papal bull named the Dum Diversas, which literally means "until different", officially condoning, sanctioning and blessing the invasion, conquest, enslavement and, in many cases, the elimination of entire populations.

"We grant you [Kings of Spain and Portugal] by these present documents, with our Apostolic Authority, full and free permission to invade, search out, capture, and subjugate the Saracens and pagans and any other unbelievers and enemies of Christ wherever they may be, as well as their kingdoms, duchies, counties, principalities, and other property [. . .] and to reduce their persons into perpetual slavery."

In effect, this was further saying that one could not be or become a Christian unless you already were a Western European Christian. Even in enslavement the Church mandated not only that the people must be converted to Christianity, but along with that conversion was the mandate to be converted to Western European culture. The consequence of refusing to do either was simply death.

And here is Matthew telling us this wondrous story of some Magi; some sorcerers, astrologers, magicians, witches, shaman following a star to come and worship the newborn Jesus as the Christ with no intention or expectation of becoming "Christian" or converting to any other faith and/or culture. They came from their own faith and culture and within the perspective of their own faith and culture they recognized that Jesus was the Christ. Oh but that we could find an inkling of that kind of open mindedness and that open heartedness in our world today either/or in our religions or in our cultures! But that is precisely why Matthew included this story in his Gospel account and that (I would presume) is why the Church endorsed this Gospel account (even if it didn't live up to the truth of its message).

This wondrous little story tells us a whole lot about Christ and it tells us a whole lot about why God came to us in Christ. Culture and religion are human inventions not divine interventions. God remains God no matter what culture and/or religion one adheres to. A culture evolves from and into social customs and norms; a group of people speaking the same language and basically doing the same things with the same attitude and priorities. Virtually all of humanity experiences God in one way or another. Humans have always had the experience and believed that there is something bigger, more powerful at the helm of creation. The essential conflict between good and evil, light and darkness permeates the human experience. We all like good things to happen to us and for us. We don't like bad things to happen to us, but good things don't always happen to us and bad things do happen to us. The essential human question is "Why and what can we do to influence this good/bad dichotomy in our favor?"

We naturally come to believe that this God is somehow behind these experiences of good and bad. When bad things happen we tend to conclude that we must have done something wrong, so we try to figure out what we did wrong and stop doing that and then we try to figure out a way to do what God wants us to do, to appease God, so that God won't do bad things to us again and God will do good things to and for us. And behold, a religion is born. THIS is what and who God is. THIS is what God wants us to do and THIS is what God doesn't want us to do and THIS is how we make God happy so God won't do bad things and will do good things to us. So we have a formula for making God happy, and we enshrine that formula in doctrines and dogmas, rituals and liturgies, which both evolve from and evolve into the social norms we call our culture.

Of course, the reality is that all together too often bad things happen to good people. Sandy Hook in Newtown is a prime and ripe example. Bad things happening are not always the work of God. After the holocaust, Neitche was right in saying that "God is dead." The assumption that God is behind all good and bad things that happen is dead. The question of good and bad, good and evil, right or wrong is removed from the realm of God and thrown forcefully onto our laps as human beings. God wants us, helps us, and empowers us to make good things happen. When bad things happen, it's not God's fault: it's the fault of human beings.

The fact of the matter is that God didn't invent Christianity; Christ didn't invent Christianity. Human beings invented Christianity to give form to what they believed God and Christ were/are all about. Unfortunately, over time Christianity joined the ranks of other religions in assuming that our religion is right and all others are wrong. Over time Christianity splintered into various denominations and sects, each claiming that their interpretation was right and all others were wrong. It is only in relatively recent history that we have begun to take ecumenicism seriously: to seriously try to understand and even more so, respect each other's positions and try to work to bring these various splinter groups back into something resembling the one body Christ calls us to be. It is only during the last two or three decades that work has begun in earnest to try to bring about similar understanding and respect between the various religions of the world so that we reclaim a sense of our common humanity above and beyond the differences between our cultures and religions that are so often the source of conflict and war.

That respect between, if not the learning about and the integration of the world's religions is very dear to my heart and I am very involved in groups working that are trying to help that happen. We have much to share with and learn from Buddhists, Hindus and many indigenous religions. I could go on about it for hours, but I've used up my allotted time for today . . . but stay tuned.

That the Magi came and found Jesus within the context of their own culture and religion is a profound statement about the true love and inclusiveness that God has for all of God's children. One does not have to don the doctrinal, dogmatic rituals and liturgies of one particular religion to know, experience and appreciate the powerful depths of that unconditional, universal love. One simply has to engage God face to face, in person, to find, feel and experience that love, and that is what the birth of Christ was and is all about.

Creator God; Creator of all, everything, everybody, you came to us and have come to us as one of us in Jesus Christ, not just to give hope, peace, love and joy to those who already believe in you, but to everybody. Your coming to us is a universal gift to all of humanity; to all of Creation.

Help us understand and be open to the possible reality that all those who claim to know you and envision you are all experiencing the same thing: YOU. The Magi came from a very different place, with a very different perspective on life, on religion, on culture, and they recognized you. Help us recognize that any person has as good a chance of recognizing you by following a star as by pondering tomes of doctrine and dogma, ritual and liturgy. You don't speak to us only in academic platitudes. You speak to us in the wonders and mysteries of simply being, being alive, being an integral part of Creation, being in wonder, being in love. Help us be open to the power of your presence in all things in the natural world, and in all things in the human world where we so often do not agree on our interpretations because we have different perspectives. Help us become open to our common perspective: you are our God and we all are your people; your children; parents and children, brothers and sisters, one to another in your love. Amen.

Prayers

Creator God; Creator of all, everything, everybody, you came to us and have come to us as one of us in Jesus Christ, not just to give hope, peace, love and joy to those who already believe in you, but to everybody. Your coming to us is a universal gift to all of humanity; to all of Creation.

Help us understand and be open to the possible reality that all those who claim to know you and envision you are all experiencing the same thing: YOU. The Magi came from a very different place, with a very different perspective on life, on religion, on culture, and they recognized you. Help us recognize that any person has as good a chance of recognizing you by following a star as by pondering tomes of doctrine and dogma, ritual and liturgy. You don't speak to us only in academic platitudes. You speak to us in the wonders and mysteries of simply being, being alive, being an integral part of Creation, being in wonder, being in love. Help us be open to the power of your presence in all things in the natural world, and in all things in the human world where we so often do not agree on our interpretations because we have different perspectives. Help us become open to our common perspective: you are our God and we all are your people; your children; parents and children, brothers and sisters, one to another in your love.

We lift up our personal joys and concerns to you, and our yearning to hear your still, small voice speaking to us, in silence . . . Amen.

Baptized With Spirit and Fire

The original meaning of baptism is simple and to the point: it means washing. Virtually every animal on earth gets clean, gets washed in one way or another. Some are rather odd, but they all serve the same purpose. Cats lick themselves. Birds preen themselves and take regular baths. Pigs get clean by wallowing in mud. Elephants do the same thing. Their skin is protected and parasites are rubbed off or washed off. Chimpanzees and other apes clean themselves in water and then and clean each other. Even creatures that live in the water have to be cleaned in one way or another. Virtually every type of animal needs cleaning and every form of cleaning has something to do with water.

It seems inherent to all creatures that they somehow know they have to be cleaned and keep clean. It's like a hygiene instinct. If you get dirty and don't do anything about it, the odds are really good that you're going to get sick. That is a simple, obvious, cause and effect observation. One didn't need to know anything about microbiology to come to that conclusion. You get dirty and stay dirty, you get sick. So people learned to wash with water.

Rubbing either rendered animal fat or an oil like olive oil on one's skin protected one's skin from the sun and served as a layer of protection against dirt. Somewhere along the way people learned that certain oils, herbs and spices not only smelled good in and of themselves, they made a person smell good when they rubbed them on their bodies. So they mixed up concoctions of oil, spices and herbs and the original perfumes came into being. When combining washing in water and then rubbing good smelling oils on yourself you end up with a pretty good smelling, clean person who is attractive to other clean, good smelling people. The first evidence of soap was found in Egyptian containers that originated about six thousand years ago, and scientists figure that soap was accidently discovered when fat dripping off a cooking animal mixed with some wood ash and somebody picked up the mixture and when they washed off they found they were really clean. Somewhere down the line somebody mixed this soap with oils, herbs and spices and people started getting really clean. Clean people are healthy people and healthy people live longer than dirty, sick people, so washing with soap and good smelling stuff helped us survive and evolve into who we are today. God's got it all figured out.

As scented oils and soaps evolved, the more and more it cost to make them. The really fancy stuff became the luxury of the rich and powerful. Ordinary people made do with that they could make for themselves. As religions came into being, the somewhat miraculous hygienic consequences of washing and rubbing good smelling oils on a person came to take on some spiritual significance. Humankind has been burning incense and making animal and vegetable sacrifices to various gods since time immemorial. Why? Well if something smells good and pleasing to us, they must also smell pretty good to God and even please God. The same holds true that if we really enjoy a piece of good, cooked meat or a really fresh loaf of bread then God must enjoy that too. So the rituals of sacrificing stuff that we really like, giving them to God, then that must please God and a happy God is much more apt to be nice to us and answer our prayers. Most every religious ritual one can name originated in some very practical, down to earth phenomenon, and baptism is no exception.

The ritual of baptism has been around for as long as human beings and religions have been around. Virtually every religion has some form of ritual washing or cleansing with water, and the intentions and the consequences of such washings go far beyond the simple cleansing of the body. They go into the realm of the cleansing of the spirit, the soul, the whole person of being a person.

One of the essential things that distinguish we human beings from other animals is that we have self consciousness. We are, to a point, objectively aware that we have a body, we have a mind, we have a heart and we have a spirit; we are a conglomeration of the physical, the mental, the emotional and the spiritual. Unlike most other animals we look in a mirror and see what we perceive to be ourselves. Having seen that, we extrapolate our self consciousness into being aware of ourselves as this quadraphonic collection of body/mind/heart/spirit; physicality/mentality/emotionalism/spirituality which was seized upon by Western European science and pseudo-science early on, and in most cases still pervades our, at least, academic perceptions of what it means to be a self; a person. My mind says this, my body says that, my heart says something else, and my spirit is somewhere else entirely. It is only recently that people have been asking and trying to understand and appreciate that, first and foremost, we are whole persons. What happens to our bodies happens to our minds, what happens to our emotions happens to our minds and bodies, what happens to our spirits happens to all of ourselves, and on and on and on until we come to realize that this quadraphonic sense of self is an illusion. We are whole beings in and of ourselves. What purports to happen and should happen in baptism is that the water washes all the dirt off your body, the guilt and confusion off of your emotions, the doubt and despair off your mind and the aloof emptiness off your spirit; again, as a whole person, all at once.

So John the Baptist set out to baptize everybody in Judea, including Jerusalem, exhorting them to repent of their sins and be cleansed of them because something dreadful was about to happen if they didn't. So who was this camel hair and leather belted locust and honey eating person, if not prophet? Remember back in Luke's account how Mary went to visit her sister Elizabeth when both of them were pregnant, under questionable circumstances, and both unborn babies jumped at their being together? The point is that Jesus and John were cousins. When they met at the river, they had known each other for their entire lives; they had grown up together; they had shared altogether who knows what, but they knew each other intimately.

When Jesus came over the hill, or down or from wherever, to the river and approached John, asking to be baptized, John's response was "I need to be baptized by you . . . but you come to me!?!?" We must pay extremely close attention to that interaction. John knew Jesus and Jesus knew John. They were not strangers. They were cousins; friends. They were spiritual kindred as well as family kindred.

When John asked Jesus why he wanted to be baptized by John, not the other way around, Jesus answered "Let it be so for now; for it is proper for us in this way to fulfill all righteousness." The reality here is that John was already recognized as someone with the spiritual authority to baptize; to clean a person spiritually; to forgive sins; to make a person acceptable to God so God would save them. John must have been recognized as some kind of priest. In those days there were the elite classes of the Chief Priests and Scribes, but there also other kinds of priests who worked more directly with the local folks, like John. We don't know much about the sect John was a part of, probably because the Church very early on did their best to distance themselves from the Jews, but the fact of the matter was that John was some kind of a Jewish priest. They didn't like the notion that Jesus or John were Jews. But what is really amazing about this story is that by baptizing Jesus, John made Jesus a Jewish priest too.

The Church calls John a prophet but no one ever prophesized anything in a vacuum. John's prophecies were respected because he was a priest. Jesus' ministry was recognized by the people because he was, in their eyes, and in their traditions, a priest. His baptism signifies the beginning of his public ministry and John baptized Jesus; John ordained Jesus into that ministry. According to their traditions, that is why Jesus allowed John to baptize him even though Jesus was, himself, the one John had been prophesying would come and be the Messiah.

John met his end when we denounced Herod for marrying his own niece, his brother's wife, implying that he had had his own brother killed so he could have his wife as his own. Herod didn't like that at all, and he probably would have killed him right off, but John was very popular with the people and Herod didn't want to incite a rebellion. He killed John later at the whim of another pretty young thing who enticed him to do so.

Herod obviously had some problems.

For such a seemingly simple story it can sure get complicated, but that's the way it is with many Bible stories. They come from different times and circumstances that can be very foreign to us, and they tend to be loaded with all kinds of baggage and hidden meanings that can be hard for us to understand.

The point remains that Jesus' baptism was the beginning of his public ministry. For the next three years or so he would preach and teach, heal people, perform miracles, and show the world that he indeed was and is the Messiah. One interesting note is that there is no direct reference to Jesus ever baptizing anyone with water, although he authorized his disciples to do so. But Jesus did indeed "baptize" everyone who heard him, believed him and had their lives changed by him, with the Holy Spirit; the zeal of the fire of the Holy Spirit that was, is and ever shall be available to all who call know Jesus to be the Christ.

Baptism obviously has many different meanings within various Christian denominations. Orthodox traditions insist that a baby be baptized as soon as possible after birth because if the child should unfortunately die before he or she was baptized they would have to go through purgatory before they could get into heaven. If a child was baptized, they and every other baptized person went straight to heaven. In our tradition baptism is more of a ritual affirming that the child or any other person is indeed a member of the body of the Church of Christ, and it is more an affirmation and commitment by the parents and the Church to raise that child and welcome that person into the body of Christ that we are.

I don't remember my baptism but my parents loved to tell the story about how I threw up on the minister while I was being baptized. Sometimes I think the rest of my life has been restitution for doing that.

Our God help us open our hearts and our minds and our whole beings that each and every moment of each and every day you offer us the help and healing, the cleansing and renewal that we identify with baptism. Baptize our bodies and make them whole and well. Baptize our hearts and make them peaceful and sensitive. Baptize our minds that we may open them to the infinity of your being. Baptize our spirits that we may be enabled to fly free in the power and presence of your love. Baptize us back into the true wholeness and wellness that we are created to be.

We pray for all who need and yearn for the power of your baptism; your help and healing; the power of your presence in their lives, and, as true disciples help become the baptizers you invite and call us to be. Amen.

The Lord's Prayer

Today I am going to talk about the history and origins of what we know as the Lord's Prayer, and before I even start, I want to make very clear the disclaimer that I in no way whatsoever am even assuming to be trying to change the way we say the Lord's Prayer. I tried that once and I wasn't sure if I was going to lose my job, my head or both, but I quickly repented of the error of my ways . . . and never brought the subject up again.

I have said before, and will say many times again; it is one thing to know what a piece of scripture says and another thing to know what it means. This is true with all literature, but it is especially true with biblical scripture because what we see as what the Bible says comes from a long process of translation, interpretation, retranslation and reinterpretation, including a great deal of editing and transliterating by any number of traditions down through the centuries. We might like to think that we can pick up a Bible and read it and those words are, word for word, exactly what the original speakers and writers were saying. Well, we can't. We have a dozen or more English versions in circulation today, which in many cases differ widely in how they translate and interpret not only the English texts of earlier versions, but all the way back to the earliest manuscripts we have in the original or near-original languages the words were first written in. Some claim to offer a high level of accurate translations, like the New Revised Standard Version we have in the pews. Some proudly proclaim that they are paraphrases of other English versions, like the Good News bible. Some argue vehemently that the version they use is the only reliable version. This is especially true of folks who use only the King James Version, quoting from the preface that it is the only ". . . authorized version of the Bible . . ." assuming that God did the authorizing, when in fact it is the only authorized version according to King James. Neither here nor there, I am not up here to argue any points pro or con, but simply to look at what the words mean, more than just what they say within our translations and our interpretations, so we all can have a better and fuller understanding of what they mean, and I include myself in that ongoing process because every time I go through the research of putting together a sermon like this, I learn something new too.

It all starts with these three simple facts: (1) The Old Testament was spoken and written in Hebrew. (2) The New Testament was written in Greek. And (3) Though Jesus and his disciples and contemporaries were certainly familiar with Hebrew and Greek the language they spoke together was Aramaic. So the earliest records of what Jesus and the disciples said are already translated from Aramaic into Greek. After that the entire Bible goes from its original languages through Latin into any number of European languages and on to what we have today.

Getting back to the Lord's Prayer, it has always somewhat amazed me that as hard as we try to develop ever more accurate and contemporary translations of the Bible, the vast majority continue to quote the Lord's Prayer, word for word, from the King James Version; Matthew 6:9-13, to be specific. Even our New Revised Standard Version does this. The reason is quite simple: TRADITION, and that, again, is not something that I would try to change, but I don't know how many times I have been challenged with serious questions, especially by children, as to what it means and why we use that language to say the Lord's Prayer. Why do some people use "debts and debtors", while others say "trespassers and trespasses" and some even say "sins and those who sin against us."? Why do the Catholics usually end the prayer with ". . . as we forgive our debtors/those who trespass against us/those who sin against us." and do not include "For thine is the kingdom and the power and the glory forever and ever. Amen." Some even say just ". . . forever. Amen", not ". . . forever and ever. Amen."? The answer, again, is TRADITION, but let's dig a little deeper into the roots of those traditions and see what might have actually been said.

The reason the Catholics use the short form, as I call it, is because they are translating directly from Luke's version of the Lord's Prayer, which except for a few ancient translations does not end with "For thine is the kingdom and the power and the glory, forever and ever. Amen" TRADITION.

I want to read you a direct translation of Luke's version from the best Greek sources we have today into relatively contemporary English.

"Our Father who is in heaven, hallowed be your name; let your kingdom come; let your will be done on earth as it also is in heaven. Give us our needed bread day by day; and forgive us our sins, for we ourselves also forgive all those indebted to us. And lead us not into temptation, but deliver us from evil. Amen."

I use Luke's version here because it is closest to what we traditionally use. Mathew and Mark's version are very different.

Matthew says, "And forgive us our debts, as we also forgiven our debtors. And do not bring us to the time of trial, but rescue us from the evil one. For if you forgive others their trespasses, your heavenly father will also forgive you; but if you do not forgive others, neither will your heavenly Father forgive your trespasses."

Mark says only, "Whenever you stand praying, forgive, if you have anything against anyone; so that your Father in heaven may also forgive your trespasses."

So a picture starts to emerge of how our version of the Lord's Prayer is actually a kind of a conglomeration of various sources, and, for me, knowing that and being aware of the other variations just enhances my understanding of what the words I am saying really mean.

In December, 2011, National Geographic Magazine published a wonderful article about the King James Version. King James had gathered the best collection he could of biblical scholars, with the best resources of ancient texts at the time, and also a number of the top literary scholars and even most recognized prose writers and poets, to not only put together an accurate translation but to form it in the best of their contemporary, common English language. I think that is one reason that the Lord's Prayer survives in that language: it is more poetic than scholarly, more prosaic than academic. It exudes an air of authority and even poetic beauty that ordinary words fail to transmit.

At the other extreme of the translations problems is the fact that Jesus spoke all these original words in Aramaic, and nobody wrote down in Aramaic what Jesus said in Aramaic, so we can only speculate what Jesus might have originally said. Fortunately we have a grand collection of other things written in Aramaic, so we know what it looked like, and there are a few enclaves in the Middle East that still speak Aramaic, so we know what it sounded like. A scholar by the name of Neil Douglas-Klotz took it upon himself to as totally as possible understand and speak and write Aramaic. This involved many years of study with Aramaic speaking people, studying their language and culture, and it all culminated in his asking this incredulous question: "What might Jesus have actually said in Aramaic, and what might it all have meant in Aramaic?" This is reverse translation. He himself admits that it is, on the bottom line, speculative, but considering his scholarly, linguistically and, dare I say the word, spiritual authority on the matter, his insight should be highly regarded and taken very seriously.

Aramaic is a VERY foreign language. It did not originate in ether the Hebrew or Greek traditions. The closest connections are languages that later developed in the various Indian and other far-middle-east areas. It was overwhelmed by the Greek-Latin languages and their protégé and for some time was considered extinct; until some explorers found those enclaves that still spoke Aramaic, which eventually enabled Neil Douglas-Klotz to do his work.

So what might have Jesus actually said and what did it all actually mean?

I am going to do something that I am pretty sure never happened in this meeting house before. From Neil Douglas-Klotz book *Prayers of the Cosmos*, I am going to read the Lord's Prayer it what might have been Jesus' original words translated into contemporary English.

O Birther! Father-Mother of the Cosmos.
Focus your light within us-make it useful:
Create your reign of unity now-
Your one desire then acts with ours,
As in all light, so in all forms.
Grant what we need each day in bread and insight.
Loose the cords of mistakes binding us,
As we release the strands we hold of others' guilt.
Don't let surface things delude us,
But free us from what holds us back.
From you is born all ruling will, the power and the life to do,
the song that beautifies all, from age to age it renews.
Truly-power to these statements-
May they be the ground from which all my actions grow: Amen.

I find it fascinating to ponder such linguistic, spiritual issues. Again, I in no way intend to change how we say the Lord's Prayer, but I do hope to enhance our appreciation of what it means.

"Amen" is the closest word we have to the original word that Jesus would have spoken. Variations on the word amen abound in many languages. The original word in Aramaic, Ameyn, means, as the author translates: "Truly—power to these statements-may they be the ground from which all my actions grow." So be it!

Transfigured or Only a Dream

The story of the transfiguration is one of those biblical stories where one must take a step back from what seems to be obvious to a place in one's heart and mind where one can acknowledge that there is much more happening here than meets the eye or the ear. Jesus invites three of his friends; his first three disciples; John, James and Peter to take a hike with him up to the top of a nearby mountain to pray. The four of them settled down to pray and suddenly Jesus looks different and he starts glowing all over. Suddenly, out of the blue, Moses and Elijah appeared and were talking to Jesus. Peter offers to set up three tents; one for Moses, one for Elijah and one for Jesus. Mark says that Jesus didn't know what to say to that because he knew that the disciples were beside themselves in fear. Other than that there is no response to Peter's offer. Suddenly, again, out of the blue, a cloud surrounds them and a voice says, "This is my beloved son, with whom I am well pleased. (The same words we heard from a cloud when Jesus was baptized, but then the voice adds) Listen to him!" Suddenly, again, Jesus is alone with his three disciples.

Quite a story to be sure; sounds more like a hallucination or a dream than a real, every day event. There is some good reason to follow that notion because all three gospel accounts emphasize that the three disciples were overcome with fear. Matthew says they so terrified they fell to the ground; they passed out and Jesus had to wake them up, saying, "Get up and do not be afraid." Luke makes a point of saying that they were exhausted but hadn't yet gone to sleep, seemingly to emphasize that this was not ". . . only a dream." Peter's offer to set up tents alludes to the probability that it was late in the day and they all needed a good night's sleep. Good old down-to-earth Peter would naturally have been that practical.

Many cultures take dreaming much more seriously than ours does. Remember back when Pharaoh was troubled by his dreams and Joseph volunteered to interpret his dreams, saying that God uses dreams to communicate with people. In the Bible there are hundreds of references to God communicating with people in dreams. Matthew emphasizes that God spoke to Joseph in a dream to stay with Mary when he had his doubts. God also spoke to Joseph in a dream he should take his family to Egypt. God spoke to the Magi in a dream telling them not to go back to Herod and to take another route home. Peter recites Joel's prophecy that ". . . your sons and your daughters shall prophesy, and the young people shall see visions, and the old people shall dream dreams." When will that happen? When God ". . . pours out God's spirit upon all flesh." That God communicates with people through dreams, visions and prophecy was a common notion among many ancient religions and still is common in some even today. Prophecy, visions and dreams have a lot in common; they all link the past with the future in the experience of our whole beings.

When we scientifically and culturally divided up ourselves into beings composed of mind, body, heart and spirit, as if we were four separate parts, we disconnected the wholeness of self that acknowledges that these four parts all work together in harmony each influencing and being influenced by; and affecting and being affected by the others. Even modern psychology recognizes that dreams are made up of wholistic memories: what we see, what we feel, what we think about, what we yearn for and/or are afraid of, and our spiritual senses all come together in dreams.

I spent a couple of years working with a Jungian Pastoral counselor after I left my last Church and was trying to figure out what to do with my life and a big part of the process was working with my dreams. The Freudian approach to dream analysis assumes that what dreams mean is the same in every person. If you see a snake in your dreams, for instance, that means the same thing as everybody else who sees a snake in their dreams. The Jungian approach is quite the opposite. Your dreams mean what they mean only to you. There may be an occasional archetype; a similar dream experience among people, but the bottom line is that your dreams are yours alone.

The first step was to adopt a discipline in which one learns to remember your dreams. Unless it is an unusually intense dream, we usually forget them when we wake up. I trained myself to remember my dreams by keeping a notepad next to my bed and when I woke up, especially in the middle of the night when I wasn't really wide awake, I would jot down a few notes about the dream I had. It was amazing how those few notes would bring back the entire dream when I did wake up and read them. Certain patterns started emerging, and I realized that I had a number of recurring dreams. To be brief, I'd like to share two of them with you. I had a recurring dream that I was walking along the shore of a raging river. I was, at the same time, very afraid of that river, but I also had the urge to jump in. My counselor suggested that the next time I had that dream to go ahead and jump in. "It's only a dream!" he laughed. So the next time I had that dream I jumped in and found myself floating in wondrously cool, refreshing water. After that, I never had that dream again. In another recurring dream I climbed to the top of a steep rocky hill and coming to the edge of the cliff at the top I looked down on a small lake. Again I was at the same time terrified, but I also had the urge to jump. The next time I had that dream it was different in that along the way as I climbed up the hill there were people in various places watching me and encouraging me, including my grandmothers and other long gone relatives. When I got to the top I spread out my arms and jumped, but I didn't fall. I flew away. After that I never had that dream again. I interpret the moral of those stories to be that when you are afraid of something that you are also attracted to, trust God, go ahead and jump, and something wondrous will happen. Sounds kind of biblical doesn't it. It should because that is what our faith is all about: facing our fears and trusting God. In that sense, I believe that God was speaking to me in my dreams.

So my point is that it doesn't matter to me whether what the three disciples experienced up there on the top of the mountain was a dream or not; if it was a practical, real time, in your face, first-hand experience or a dream. To me both are equally real and valid. What matters is what the experiences meant to them, and so, what they can mean to us. "And while he was praying, the appearance of his face changed and his clothes became dazzling white." Was that something supernatural; something mystical; something miraculous? The point is that for the first time the disciples saw Jesus to be who he really was (and is): the Christ in all his glory. He was transfigured not just *before* their eyes but *in* their eyes. The appearance of Moses and Elijah was an affirmation that Jesus was the real thing, right up there on if not above a par with the two greatest people of faith in all their history.

"Just as they were leaving . . ." Peter offers to set up some tents for them so they could stick around for a while. Peter wanted to spend some time with them; learn from them; experience them. They couldn't do that. After all, this was ". . . only a dream." Then a bright cloud envelops them and the real meaning of the story unfolds. Again God says "This is my beloved Son with whom I am well pleased" and drives it all home with the admonition: "Listen to him!" In the end Jesus is transfigured *in* our eyes; *in* our whole beings, when we listen to him.

Do not be afraid to look deep into someone's face; in someone's countenance and see the holiness that is there.

Our God help us allow you to be transfigured in our whole being; in how we see you, in how we hear you, in how we think about you, in how we feel you. Help us embrace your dazzling glory in all the ways we can experience you. Help us expect to have experiences of you that are far beyond what we expect; help us expect surprises; help us expect miracles; help us expect to be transfigured not just in our experiences of you but by you as you enable us to become the holy persons you see us as and call us to be.

You know everything there is to know about each and every one of us. You know what fears we harbor that hold us back from letting go in our faith and letting you be who you are: the helper, healer, the teacher, the visionary, the prophet, the dreamer, the totally faithful one in whose image you create us to be.

We pray that where we are broken you will make us whole; where we are ill or injured in any part of our beings you will heal us; where we are afraid you will give us unfailing faith and the confidence to go ahead and jump; where we feel lost and alone you will give us comfort and companionship. And we pray that you make of us the helpers and healers, the prophets and dreamers, the loving and loved sons and daughters you call us to be. Amen.

To The End Of The Age

Back in the days of the psalmists chariots and horses were the contemporary equivalent of a weapon of mass destruction; a true instrument of terror. The horses were trained to trample anything and anyone in their path. Swords were mounted pointing out from the spokes of the chariots wheels so, like a giant combination lawn mower and steam roller, the whole thing was a very efficient killing machine, truly due to be feared by anyone in their path, and yet trusted, even boasted about (as some translations render it) by those who rode them.

Nobody knows for sure if David wrote all the psalms that are attributed to him. It's much more likely that many of these psalms were dedicated to David, but whoever or whatever it was an extremely bold claim to trump the mighty power and terror of chariots with and warhorses trusting (even boasting) in the name of our God: the Most High.

In times such as we have been going through as of late, between Sandy Hook, the bombings at the Boston Marathon and the ensuing equally tragic manhunt we face off against people who trust in guns and bombs to do their terrible bidding, instead of chariots and horses, but we find ourselves challenged to having to ask ourselves if we can or do really trust our God, the Most High. Our faith in the sovereignty of God is challenged. The fact is that it tends to take only more guns and bombs to stop those who trust in guns and bombs and we spiral down into a chaos of violence and terror begetting more violence and terror and on and on and on. The wars in Korea, Viet Nam, Iraq, Afghanistan, Pakistan, and elsewhere in the Middle East and in various corners of our world are all proof positive that we are caught up in this downward and seemingly escalating spiral of violence and terror. We no longer have two distinct armies facing each other on a battle field, who go at it killing and wounding each other until one side surrenders and the war is over. In today's wars there never is a definitive victory or defeat. There is primarily just cessation of the conflict due to attrition either by the number of people killed and wounded or one side simply runs out of money. The reasons behind the conflicts and wars are rarely if ever addressed and even more rarely dealt with and reconciled.

On the home front it is an equally downward spiral. Sales of all sorts of weapons and ammunition skyrocketed after Sandy Hook and the twisted rumors that our government was going to somehow turn into a dictatorship and take all our guns away by force, if necessary, started surfacing. Guns beget guns beget guns; bombs beget bombs beget bombs; violence begets violence begets violence; profit begets profit begets profit and the fact that our fractured, fragmented and polarized government can't even begin to get a handle on what to do about it; to help the situation, just illustrates how far we have fallen in our downward spiral into obsession with guns, bombs and violence as well as deceptions, as well as downright lies.

Joshua challenges the fledgling people of Israel: "Now if you are unwilling to serve the Lord; if you are unwilling to serve Yahweh; if you are unwilling to serve God, then choose this day who you will serve." As Bob Dylan so eloquently sings, "You gotta serve somebody. It may be the devil or it may be the Lord, but you gotta serve somebody." Joshua concludes his challenge by saying, "As for me and my house we will serve the Lord; Yahweh; God." Who or what have we been forced to choose between?

Getting back to the names of God, there is really only one formal name for God and that is a name that was forbidden to be spoken by the Hebrews and Israelites, so in Hebrew we only find four consonants and no vowels. All we have is the equivalent of YHWH. Scholars have made very educated guesses that when spoken it would have probably been something like YaHWeH; Yahweh which is a broadly encompassing name that means, all at once, I AM/I WAS/I WILL BE; I AM THE SOURCE OF ALL THAT HAS EVER BEEN AND EVER WILL BE INCLUDING ALL OF EXISTENCE AND LIFE. That is God's name according to Hebrew traditions, but there are many names that describe God, including El Elyon (El is God, Elyon is Most High), El Shaddai (God almighty); El Olam (everlasting God); El Hal (living God); El Roi (God of seeing) and the list goes on and on. This makes a lot of sense from our perspective. We can say the name "God" or "Yahweh" but we have to go to great lengths to describe what we mean by those names. They are not self explanatory, so in order to convey what we mean by "God" we have to have all these ways of describing God: Creator, Sustainer, Redeemer, Father/Son/Holy Spirit (or as I like to say: Father, Child and Mother), and on and on and on. Theological and liturgical libraries are filled to the brim with tomes about what we try to mean when we say the word "God."

As Christians we have a unique perspective when it comes to describing what we mean by God. We have a person to turn to. What do we mean by God? Just take a look at Jesus; listen to Jesus; hear his words of justice, righteousness, hope, peace and love. That's what we mean when we talk about God. There is no question that many images of God found in the Old Testament are changed by Jesus' New Testament images of God. The angry, wrathful images of God are gone, replaced by the loving and gracious images of God that we find in Jesus. We can return the imagery about having to fear God to its original intent; the Hebrew word for "fear" is more accurately translated as "respect". We should translate the words of the Wisdom literature (Ecclesiastes, Proverbs, the Song of Solomon, and others) as "Respect for God is the beginning of Wisdom." not "Fear of God is the beginning of Wisdom."

How we perceive God and how we talk about God has everything to do with how we perceive and talk about life in general. If we perceive God as being angry and wrathful we will probably deal with life in angry and wrathful ways. We stand in shock wondering how some Muslims can interpret parts of the Koran as giving license if not orders to be angry and wrathful at any and all non-Islamic believers. The fact of the matter is that very similar words exist in parts of our own Old Testament, and pulled out of context there have been many examples down through history of Christians believing and acting as if it was their divine duty to persecute if not annihilate any and all non-Christian believers. The Crusades are the prime example. Colonialism and slavery are other prime examples, both of which were perfectly justified by the then Orthodox Church: the one and only True Church.

The key words here are ". . . pulled out of context . . ." The love and grace we find in Christ are totally incompatible with the notion that we are called to persecute or annihilate anyone who does not agree with just how and what we believe. Contrary to many fundamentalist perspectives the Bible is not a literal translation of the Word of God. God is not limited to or by any particular language which we, as human beings most certainly are. There is no such thing as a literal interpretation of the Bible. "Literal interpretation" is a contradiction in terms. Every translation is an interpretation in and of itself. The Bible often contradicts itself as between the images of God being angry and wrathful and the images of God being loving and gracious, but they also illustrate the contradictions be encounter in life. This is what happens when you believe in and serve an angry and wrathful God. This is what happens when you believe in and serve a loving and gracious God. God doesn't change, but certainly our perceptions of God can and do.

Again, as Christians we have (or should have) a unique perspective on all these issues. We do (or should) believe in and endeavor to serve a loving and gracious God. There is no place in our faith for imagery of an angry and wrathful God. If God got angry at and wrathful towards those who thwart or deny God's will, there would be no Holocausts, or Columbines, or Sandy Hooks, or Marathon bombers. Certainly none of those events are part of God's loving and gracious will and we unavoidably end up asking the awful and unanswerable question "Why?"

"Why?" can only be answered by the truth that God created us with freedom of choice because the fact of the matter is that both evil and good are real and life is a constant challenge to ". . . choose this day who or what you will serve . . ." When somebody casts the words of the Bible in stone and pulls bits and pieces of it out of context to serve their own ends we are denied a choice in the matter. They claim to be absolutely right, so any deviation is absolutely wrong. This was true with slavery, oppression of women and more persecutions and oppressions that we can count; all of which were justified by the Bible by the interpreters of their day. The bottom line, in your face, stone cold reality is that faith is a choice. We are given the choice between an angry and wrathful God and a loving and gracious God.

One might think that the choice would be obvious. One would always want love and grace for themselves and their immediate loved ones, but again we are so caught up in our spirals of anything-but-love-and-grace; anger, violence, aggression and persecuting prejudices that it is very difficult to really embrace the love and grace we can find in God. When people have made ungracious and unloving choices that effect our lives it is very difficult to "turn the other cheek" so to speak, and sometimes we have to defend ourselves against that other slap. It's not easy to believe this with all our hearts, minds and strength to be sure, but that is what our faith is/should be all about.

The choice as to what one believes is not just an academic or logical decision. It is a wholistic decision; it is a spiritual decision. We must decide to open ourselves to the love and grace of God; to put the love and grace of God to work in our lives and see what happens. We must choose to let God be God and try to live our lives as our loving and gracious God wants us to and believe that God can and will make it happen.

So this brings us back around to the resurrection. The resurrection assures that if we entrust ourselves to the love and grace of God and if we put them to work in our lives God will make them happen in our lives and among us all and all people everywhere.

I chose Matthew's version of the resurrection for today's scripture reading because in comparison to the others it is simple, direct and to the point. Jesus appears to the disciples, empowers them to live in and by the love and grace of God and they/we are told get out there and get to work. But he doesn't simply disappear. He simply says what the heart and soul of the resurrection is all about. He simply says "I will be with you until the end of the age"; words that can also be accurately translated as "I will always be with you." That is our hope; that is our faith and that is what can get us through days and weeks like last week, and weeks before, and weeks to come and that is what can prepare us and enable us to get to work and make God's love and grace real for everybody; ourselves included. Christ is always with us.

Our loving and gracious God, we lift up to you all the victims of last week's acts of terror and violence; all those who were killed and their families and friends; all those who were wounded in their bodies and face major life changes; all those who were and are wounded in the shattering of celebration, peace and trust into fear and paranoia and just plain worry.

We grieve for the victims of those and all the acts of meaningless, mindless and horrific violence that we have experienced in our lives and down through history, and in truth we grieve for ourselves and each other as we find our faith is challenged; our trust is challenged, not only in each other and other peoples, but in you.

Why didn't you prevent these horrific acts from happening? People have been asking you that question for all of human history. People have shut you out of their lives because they don't like the absence of an obvious answer, or they just don't accept the answer you set before us. God and evil are real but it is our choice who we will serve

You set before us the ways of life and death, good and evil, darkness and light and ask US to choose. The choice should be obvious, but it is so marred and tangled up in our webs of prejudice and anger and violence that it can be very hard to make a real choice. Help us choose the paths of faith: the paths of opening ourselves to the power and the presence of your love and grace. Help us choose and open ourselves to the truth of the resurrection; Christ's resurrection; our resurrection; your resurrection; the resurrection of hope in the face of despair; light in the face of darkness; life itself in the face of death; love in the face of hate, anger and violence; peace in the face of strife and war.

Our God we tend to be somewhat overloaded with worries at times like these. Help us acknowledge and heal our worries, but also help us celebrate our joys. Amen.

GONE FISHIN'

Enough was enough. They had been in hiding for who knows how many days. They were tired of being sacred. They were bored to tears. Enough was enough. After all, Jesus was dead and buried; their wonderful new life was over and done; dead and gone just like Jesus. Good old thick as a brick but solid as a rock Simon Peter broke the ice. "I've had it. I'm going back to my old life. I'm going fishing." So the old gang of fishermen who had left their nets in the first place to follow Jesus: Simon (now Peter), Andrew, James, John and a couple other disciples who didn't have anything better to do, tacked a sign on the door saying "Gone Fishin'" and they headed back up to the Sea of Tiberias, where it all began, loaded up their boat and headed out to sea to catch some fish.

Back in those days and in plenty of places around the world still today fishing was done at night. They had a bright torch or lamp or lantern that attracted the fish. They threw their nets into the water, hung the light on a long pole so it was right over the net and when the fish came to the light they pulled the net up from underneath the fish and hauled them into the boat. If they were lucky they'd catch enough fish right off the bat and it would be a short night's work. If they weren't lucky they could be out there all night. It was strenuous work and it was wet work. Between the sweat and the water they'd strip down the bare essentials so their clothes wouldn't get dirty and wet.

Well, that night they weren't lucky at all. Cold and tired; between their depression and despair over Jesus' death and the end of that whole adventure and their frustration over not catching any fish they were a pretty ornery crew. Everybody knows how ornery a frustrated fisher-person can be, and the last thing they want to hear in that condition was any dumb questions or any unwanted advice.

About dawn, as the skies started lighting up a mist or fog would form on the surface of the water. They couldn't see the shore, but obviously someone could see them; someone who asked the dumb question "Catch any fish?" to which in unison they growled out a nasty "No!" A couple of minutes later they got some unwanted advice "Try the other side of the boat." John didn't record the conversation among the fisherman that followed; probably rightly so, but in the end someone, maybe even Peter said "What the heck, let's give it a try; we've got nothing left to lose." They threw out the net and hauled it up to the surface and it full of so many fish that by rights the net should have been torn apart; but it wasn't. There so many fish they couldn't haul it up into the boat. They would have to drag it with the boat to shore to unload it.

About now they were getting kind of curious. All of this was strangely familiar; more than a touch of déjà-vu; been here, done this. They all stopped what they were doing and stared into the mist to try to see who it was there on the shore. One of the disciples finally said, "I think it is the Lord!" At that good old thick as a brick but solid as a rock Peter had again had enough, so he pulls out his clothes from where he had stowed them to keep them dry; pulls them on and dives into the water and starts sprint swimming the hundred yards to shore. The rest of them stayed with their ship and rowed the boat, hauling the overflowing net full of fish towards shore. Peter finally made it to shore and crawled on his hands and knees up the sand, looking for all the world like a drowned rat; his mouth hanging open and his eyes bugging out as he recognized who it was there on the shore. Jesus says, "Bring me some of the fish you just caught and we'll have breakfast." At that Peter says something like, "Um . . . er . . . OK boss.", turns around dives back into water, sprint swims back to the boat and personally hauls the whole thing; boat, net full of fish and the other fisher folk into shore.

Now they are all looking like drowned rats, their mouths hanging open and their eyes bugging out, as they recognized who it was there on the shore. Jesus had already prepared a charcoal fire and had some bread and fish already cooking on it. "Come on . . . let's have some breakfast." Then Jesus passed around the bread and the fish and they ate it in dumbfounded silence. Nobody said a word, but I'll bet Jesus had a funny little smile on his face. As John puts it, none of them dared to ask who he was because they all knew it was the Lord; none of them dared NOT to believe he was the Lord.

I don't usually play favorites, but this is my favorite resurrection story, and it's my favorite because it is so HUMAN; it's so real; it paints a poetic picture in which one can visualize and sensualize the whole scene. You can smell the sea air, feel the cool, damp night, hear the wind in the rigging, smell the charcoal fire and the bread and fish cooking on it, see the mist hanging over the water in the dawn light. You can see the dumbfounded looks on the faces of the disciples. This was the last thing any of them expected.

Often times it is very difficult to get a handle on the humanness of the people being talked about. They are aloof, painted in words that make them very difficult to relate to; they are too pious, too superhuman, too composed and that tends to make us feel inferior in relation to them. Some of this is intentional editing I am sure. The writers wanted to portray the characters as something more than ordinary mere mortals and to be sure the characters did some pretty amazing things, but the point remains that the Bible was written about human beings, by human beings and for human beings especially when it comes to the story of Christ and Christ's resurrection. The whole intent is to point out that he was a real human being just like us.

Actually most of the stories of the resurrection are intentionally emphasizing the humanness of the whole situation. You can see Mary's tears; you can feel her reaching out to hold him. Two of the disciples were just walking down the road when they encountered Jesus but didn't recognize him. Thomas had to touch his wounds in order to believe. The point the writers were pushing was to emphasize that all of this was real in a very human way. Jesus himself points out that ghosts don't have flesh and bones and they don't need to eat. The stories are intentionally holistically sensual; you can feel; you can experience what was going on there.

Our traditions tend to present the bible characters as being somehow superhuman and that separates them from us in a way that gets in the way of the message that is trying to be conveyed. Simon Peter is a prime example. He really was thick as a brick but solid as a rock. In a number of situations in the gospels he simply didn't get what Jesus was trying to teach. In one situation Jesus actually called him Satan and told him to get out of Jesus' way. Peter swore that he would rather die than deny him, but he did so three times. Jesus asks him in the same question three times, "Do you love me?" Peter answers emphatically three times, "Yes I Do . . . Yes I love you . . . you know everything; you know that I love you!" Jesus counters three times, "tend my sheep . . . feed my lambs . . . feed my sheep." It is Peter: thick as a brick but solid as a rock; it is Peter in all his humanness that Jesus said to him, "You are the rock upon which I will build my Church." which led the Orthodox Church to assume that Peter was the first Pope and all Popes are the spiritual descendants of Peter.

The Gospels didn't happen nor were they intended to be presentations of a superhuman story about superhuman people, but that is the way they have often been interpreted and presented. Quite the contrary they happened and they were intended to present the reality of the love and grace of God; the reality of the Good News (which is what the word Gospel actually means) to us everyday ordinary people just like you and me and everybody else.

A few years back a song came out called "What If God Was One of Us" by Joan Osborne and my daughters got me a copy of it saying I think you're really going to like this Dad, and I did and I do. I'd like to share the words with you.

If God had a name what would it be?
And would you call it to his face?
If you were faced with him
In all his glory
What would you ask if you had just one question?
What if God was one of us?
Just a slob like one of us
Just a stranger on the bus
Trying to make his way home
If God had a face what would it look like?
And would you want to see
if seeing meant that
you would have to believe
in things like heaven and in Jesus and the saints
and all the prophets
What if God was one of us?
Trying to make his way home
Back up to heaven all alone
Nobody calling on the phone
'cept for the Pope maybe in Rome.

We tend to envision God in human terms: in our culture we tend to envision an old man with the long flowing white hair and beard. Other cultures envision God as different looking people, but the intent is the same. It is natural that we do this: we envision things in images that are familiar to us. Certainly one of the reasons that God presented us with Christ is that we can relate to a person, identify with a person. We can run into trouble sometimes though if we go too far at envisioning God in human terms and we impose our human limitations on God. God is ultimately a mystery; God is so much more than we can imagine or envision and it's good to embrace God as a mystery; to let God be God even if we don't or can't fully understand God. Maybe we can't fully understand God, but God most certainly fully understands us and God's one and only response to our humanness is love and grace.

So keep your eyes and ears open. God might well be that voice in the mist asking "Catch any fish?" and if we haven't God will give us some simple advice: "Try the other side of the boat." God might be that stranger on the bus. Good questions . . . good advice.

God help us let you be a mystery; our God of love and grace, but also our God who continually surprises us. As our Creator and Sustainer you are indeed in everything inanimate and alive. Help us open our eyes and see you and your loving grace in all things, in all beings, in all people.

Help us expect to be surprised; help expect to hear your voice in the mist asking us how we are doing? Help us open our ears and hear your advice and help us take your advice to heart and let it happen; let it change us; let it help us grow into the people you want us to be.

We pray for ourselves and each other: the worries we carry around with us, the fears that hold us down, the illnesses and injuries we endure in body, mind heart and soul. Assure us up and out of our worries; set us free to fly high and free in the power of the presence of your love and grace; help us and heal us in all the ways we need to be healed. Amen.

Sing a New Song

I don't know about all of you, but I sure am ready for some serious springtime: warmth, more daylight, plants and trees erupting in blossoms and green, blossoming flowers erupting in multi-beautiful-colors and a myriad of wondrous and invigorating fragrances. The first thing that just about all plants and animals do in the spring is procreate, make seeds, set fruit, have babies all setting the stage for even more plants and animals yet to come. Surely Spring is all about singing a new song and God invites us to sing along.

It's not just that I do not enjoy winter. The first snow storms are a cause for celebration in their own right, but I get tired of the shortening days and the deepening cold and just putting up with the hassle of dealing with snow and ice, as well as continuously loading the wood stove and enduring its occasional inadequacies. I like to tell the story of how when I lived up in the North Country winter would set in right after Thanksgiving and it stayed that way until sometime in March. When I lived in Bangor the temperature would drop below zero right about Christmastime and it would stay below zero until sometime in late January or even early February. All the bars and restaurants would have special celebrations when it got above zero for the first time. I moved up there in the late summer and I was curious about why all the roads had really wide shoulders along side of them. Well, come late winter those shoulders were piled head-or-more high with snow plowed in, up, on and over them.

Of course, up there one celebrated the end of winter with the advent of bogging down in mud-season and just when it gets warm enough to do something outside the black flies come back to life too and they are hungry and they are thirsty and they are nasty. Planting the garden meant climbing into what amounted to a suit of armor: long sleeves, long pants with rubber bands sealing up all the cuffs, heavy gloves and a head net securely tucked into a well buttoned up collar, serious doses of Deet and other toxic chemicals liberally applied, until somebody discovered that Avon's "Skin So Soft" was a very effective black fly and other bugs repellant. Sales soared; they now have dozens of applications as bug repellents; and it smells good! But, that's the way it was up there and you just had to get used to it. Down here winter comes and goes and comes and goes; there is no time or reason to really get used to it.

Joni Mitchell wrote a song a number of years' back called "The Circle Game" and this is the refrain:

> "And the seasons they go 'round and 'round
> And the painted ponies go up and down
> We're captive on the carousel of time
> We can't return, we can only look behind
> From where we came
> And go round and 'round and 'round
> In the circle game."

Yep, the seasons do go round and round and sometimes the transitions are causes for great relief and celebration, like winter turning into spring, and sometimes they are cause for melancholy like when the beautiful leaves of Fall turn brown and fall off and all the colors fade to black, brown, grey and white and winter begins to set in. For all we complain about the cold, in a few weeks we'll all be complaining about the heat. That's just the way it is. We gotta get used to it. The Good News is that each and every change of season is, in effect, God singing a new song and asking us to join in; inviting us to sing a new song too.

I don't know about all of you, but I'm ready for some relief from winter. I'm also more than ready for some relief from the winter of massacres, bombings, wars and other senseless acts of violence, anger, hate and biased, prejudiced animosity as well as indifference and apathy. The Good News is that here again, God is continually trying to teach us a new song and invites us to sing along with God. Every season comes with its' own joys and sorrows; every season of the year and every season of life, and every season of our personal, familial, communal, local, regional, national and international lives. Good stuff happens and bad stuff happens, but again, the Good News is that God is not resigned to those cycles of good and bad stuff. God's intent, God's promise that is that we will all sing a new song and God is constantly, ceaselessly trying to teach us a new song and this new song is a song of hope and in this season of our nation and our world we desperately need a new song of hope!

The other day I was driving along and happened upon a purportedly popular talk show host whose megalomaniacal message of the moment was that massacres and bombings and wars and other senseless acts of violence, anger, hate and biased, prejudiced animosity as well as indifference and apathy are always going to be there; they're always going to happen, so we gotta get used to them. I almost drove off the road! Well, I'm not going to get used to them because God refuses to get used to them. Getting used to them is essentially letting the terrorists win, and by terrorists I do not mean exclusively Islamic Jihadists, but by every person who wields their personal, political and religious agendas by intimidation if not by force. God's not about to get used to all that and neither am I and neither should we as the Church of Jesus Christ; the Church of God.

Jesus himself said things like "There will always be wars and rumors of wars . . ." or "The poor will always be with you . . ." But he didn't mean for us to resign ourselves to war and the poor, like "Get used to it." What Jesus meant was that because there are wars and rumors of war and the poor are indeed always with us we constantly have our work cut out for us. Jesus is NOT saying "Get used to it." Jesus IS saying "Get to work." giving all people a new song to sing.

God is continually and ceaselessly singing a new song and God invites us to join in at every turn in the road or at every turn of the season. God's new song is actually a song that is old as all time, space, being, and existence. It's the same song that God sang at the beginning of Creation and will still be singing at the end. It's the same song that God's always been singing: love and grace, love and grace from God to us and hopefully, if we can learn the song, from us to each other. God's trying to teach us the song of love and grace and for most of us in the face of the winters of the world; it really is a new song!

Communion is one stanza in this new song. We celebrate that we are one with Christ and one with each other. We celebrate putting on a new body and filling ourselves with new life giving blood. We celebrate that we have been invited to sing this new song and we have joined the choir.

All God's critters got a place in the choir. Some sing low, some sing higher, some sing out loud on the telephone wire, and some just clap their hands or paws or anything they got now.

Let us join in the heavenly chorus and sing a new song.

Our God teach us your new/old song, the one you have always been singing and always will be singing until we all catch the tune and join in. Help us sing your song of love and grace even in the face of darkness, doubt and despair. Help us sing your song of love and grace for everyone to hear and believe and join in.

Spring reminds us that no matter how harsh the winter may have been, under the snow and ice life was waiting and preparing for your warmth and light to arouse them and come to blossom and send forth new shoots of life into the world. Help us do the same thing: help us bring renewal and abundant beauty and joy into being for all people. We know it's all there inside each and every one of us just waiting for spring to come. Make spring come within and among all people everywhere. Shine the warmth and light of your love and grace on us, within us and among us for all to see and share in. Amen.

"... AND THEY ALL UNDERSTOOD EACH OTHER..."

The word Spirit in English covers a lot of ground. We find it in the words inspire, inspiration, the spire of a Church. Originally, in Hebrew and Aramaic the word is "Rhuach" which literally means wind or breath. In Greek the word is "pneuma", which we use in the pneumatic tools for instance: air tools. Both are very breathy words: rooooahhhhhc; newwwmahhh"; indicative of the breath and wind of the Spirit. In Latin the word is "spirit" from which derive our Spirit. In Genesis where it says that the Spirit of God was moving over the face of the waters it literally means that the breath of God or the wind of God was blowing on the face of the waters. The origins of the word Spirit are very practical. What's the difference between a living being and a dead being? A living being has breath; a dead being doesn't. It was a common understanding that breath was the source of life. Like wind you can certainly feel breath; you can smell wind and breath and see its effects, but the wind itself is invisible. It's a good metaphor for the Spirit of God: you can certainly see its effects, but the Spirit itself is invisible. A powerful image of the Spirit of God is also found in smoke and fire; the wind blows the smoke and fire around but you can't see the wind. Incense has long been associated with the Spirit of God. Fire starts the smoking which disperses the wonderful smell of the incense.

Virtually every religion has at its roots some image of the invisible but ever present presence of the divine; something much greater than ourselves and though we can again certainly feel and see and otherwise sense its presence and effects we can't see it. In our tradition the Gospel of John says that Jesus said "God is spirit, and those who worship Him must worship in spirit and truth." It's interesting to note that he didn't say God is **A** Spirit, as if God is one spirit among many.

At the core of our tradition is the faith that there is only one God and God exists as Spirit, so as there is only one God there is only one Spirit.

It's also interesting to note that Hebrew and Aramaic are very gender specific: every noun is definitely either male or female, and Rhuach is definitely female, which is where we get the inclusive notion that the original meaning of the Trinity was not simply Father, Son and Holy Spirit, but Father, Child and Mother, but that's another theme for another sermon.

So here we have room full of people from all over the place who are celebrating the Hebrew celebration and feast of Pentecost. The word Pentecost is a transliteration of the Greek word Pentecostos which literally means "fifty" and refers to the feast that was held fifty days after the first harvest of grain after the Passover. Originally it was probably a fertility ritual celebrating the first harvest of the Spring so indeed it was a feast. It was adapted to the Hebrew traditions, and even today Pentecost is celebrated roughly fifty days after Easter.

So all these people from all over the place, speaking all sorts of different languages, eating and drinking and having a real party when all of a sudden, literally from out of the blue, the house and everybody in it is blasted by this powerful wind that comes out of nowhere, and if that's not crazy enough riding the wind are these tongues of fire that alight on every person in the place, and if that's not crazy enough after the wind and the fire everybody starts gibber-jabbing in languages they never ever heard of, and even more miraculous than that, they all of a sudden can understand each other; they can understand each other's words in their own languages.

Now some interpretations of all of this maintain that they were speaking in an entirely new language; glossolalia as the Pentecostals would say, and they insist that people can still "speak in tongues" speak in this new language if they allow the Holy Spirit to inspire them do so. Personally I think they are missing the point.

The miracle of all of this, if you will, is not that they spoke some new common language, but that they could quite simply understand each other in whatever language they spoke. It's like the story of the Tower of Babel in reverse. In that story which explains how it came to be that people speak so many different languages, the assumption is that once upon a time everybody spoke the same language so they all got together to build a tower that would reach all the way up into heaven where they expected to find God. God didn't like that idea much so he confounded the people by giving them each a different language to speak, none of which anybody else could understand. Being so confounded by not understanding each other they couldn't cooperate enough to build the tower. This story also explains why people of different languages have such a hard time cooperating about anything at all.

The story of Pentecost begins with people not being able to understand each other. It also starts with the situation that here they are all gathered together to share in a feast celebrating the goodness of God and in that setting the Spirit of God comes upon them and they can understand each other. The issue at hand here is not just a linguistic problem; it's not just about the words they spoke, but in the deeper language of faith, if you will, in which we certainly can understand each other.

Consider the United Nations in which people from all over the world gather to solve international problems. They gather to cooperate and work for the common good among all nations and all people. They gather to overcome their confoundedness. They don't all speak the same language and they don't have to. They all have their translators but they are speaking a common language that goes far beyond the written or spoken word. I think the same is true about our coming together in the life of our faith working together to realize the will of God which is, quite simply, to be as loving and gracious with each other as God is with us. God then essentially becomes our translator and we are able to understand each other and work together despite the fact that we speak different languages.

This sort of thing happens all the time. Groups from Churches, Synagogues, Mosques and all sort of religious and secular organizations go to faraway places to do work projects of one kind or another and though they don't speak the same language, they speak the common language of good will and helping each other. They don't need to speak the same language, but if they stay together long enough they will eventually learn each other's language. I went to Puerto Rico for ten days in my senior year of high school and learned more Spanish there than I learned in four years of classes in high school.

The language of the love and grace of God is understood by everyone. Everyone wants to live long, healthy, happy, loving, and fulfilled lives. What confounds us is that we tend not to realize that we really do need each other's help in making that happen, and so often it's our languages that get in the way of that happening. The languages of our religions, our doctrines and dogmas, our political and economic policies confound our most basic human needs because though we may wish for all that makes life good, we forget or ignore the fact that all others wish for the same.

In God's Spirit God offers us a new language to speak: the language of the love and grace of God and when we listen to each other in that language we can and do understand each other.

The presence of the Holy Spirit rounds out the doctrine of the Trinity, which is just a metaphor for three of the ways we encounter God. In Creation we encounter God the Creator (or Father or Mother or both). In person we encounter God in Jesus Christ (the Son (the Child). We also encounter God in ways and words that go far beyond mere linguistic description; in ways we can feel and smell and listen to though we cannot see it itself. That's what the Holy Spirit is all about; the living, loving breath and wind of God. All together we encounter the one God. I like to say that I appreciate the metaphorical even poetic imagery of the doctrine of the Trinity, but I do not take it literally. There is only one God who we encounter and experience in many ways.

When we open ourselves to the power of the presence of God all around us, within us and among us, we encounter the one and the same God in many ways, but it all adds up to one. When we open ourselves to the love and grace of God and seek to share it with others, God is our interpreter and we can all come to understand each other as the brothers and sisters we all are to each other

Prayers

Our God, help us open ourselves to the power of your presence within us, among us and all around us. Come roaring into our lives like a blast of mighty wind. Purify and temper us with the fire of your love. Fill us to overflowing with your Spirit of life, love, beauty and grace. Breathe on us, breathe through us enlivening our lives and our life together with the truth that all people, all life, all existence is the Creation of your Spirit.

Our God, help us come to truly understand each other. Help us look beyond all that seems to confound, confuse and keep us apart. Help us truly know, understand and believe that we are indeed all your children, created and loved by you more than we know; that we are indeed all brothers and sisters and all should be treated accordingly. Bust open our closed hearts and minds and truly understand, while still acknowledging that above and beyond all we can understand you remain the ultimate mystery. Like a parent you create us; like a brother or sister you came to us in person; like a breath of fresh wind and cleansing fire you are here among us and within us all. Amen.

In Memory of Peace

May 26, 2013

On Memorial Day we remember, honor and give thanks to and for all the men and women who served, suffered and died in all of the conflicts, wars and rumors of wars that we have endured (and are enduring) in order to become a nation and to survive as a nation. This includes all our allies and all the victims of these wars, including children, who were caught in the cross fire. Jesus himself said that there will always be wars and rumors of war, but in the next breath he says that he came and comes to give us peace; peace which passes all understanding.

    I know that in one sense he is talking about inner peace; peace which one can have inside oneself even the midst of conflicts and wars as well as all times of stress, worry and fear. I remember clearly the night during the Cuban missile crisis when I was awakened by the thunder of B52s coming into Bradley airport which was used as a staging area in preparation for a possible attack either on or from Cuba and/or the Soviet Union. I knew those planes were carrying nuclear weapons and as a child of the cold war I was well versed in what nuclear weapons could do. I went and sat with my mother in the living room and asked if we were going to war and if we were going to die. Even back then I knew that very few people on either side would survive if we engaged in a nuclear war. She said she really didn't know but at times that like you have to trust God and take things one day at a time. I knew that she and my father had been separated for years when he was serving in the Army in the Pacific theater, as they called it, and the only way they got through it was to trust God and take things one day at a time. That comforted me and gave me peace.

That's as close as I ever got to war. I registered with the Selective Service as a Conscientious Objector during the Viet Nam war, even though they called it a conflict. I was granted that status and was prepared to do two years of alternative service, but in the end my lottery number never came up. I was an antiwar activist during those years, but my focus was not just on the anti-Viet Nam war but on all war, strife and violence in general, and that is still my ideal today, but my idealism has been tempered by the realities of our very complex, conflicting and confounding world. Actually the closest I ever got to combat was when I was in North Carolina and a bunch of us long haired hippies were sitting next to a pond off campus and some of the locals came up on a hill behind us and started firing their rifles over our heads into the pond.

I have many friends who served in Viet Nam, but I never took on the attitude that they did something wrong by doing do. Most of them were drafted and they simply obeyed orders. I have other friends who refused to be drafted and spent two years in jail for doing so. I have one friend who was seriously wounded in Viet Nam, spent years recovering and has had a very difficult time with post-traumatic-stress-disorder. He works with other veterans as part of his therapy and now seeing all these people coming back from the Middle East in as bad a shape as he was, if not worse, has set him back a long way in dealing with his own PTSD. He likes to say that the wounds to his body are not the problem; it's the wounds in his soul that won't heal. He is still searching for his own inner peace.

I have much older friend who had a PhD in chemistry and at the beginning of WW II chose to serve in a military weapons research center instead of going into the military. He was sent to a top secret weapons center in Rocky Mount, Tennessee and was told that once he entered that compound he could not leave until the project was completed and he could have no contact with the outside world whatsoever for the duration. After a while he caught on that they were inventing the atomic bomb and when he voiced his opposition to such a terrible weapon he was told that if he refused to continue his work he would be immediately drafted into the Army, he would be ordered to continue his work and if he still refused he would be formally charged and convicted by a courts martial and would probably spend the rest of his life in jail. He reluctantly but honorably finished his work and on the day the war ended he quit his job, went back to school, got another PhD, this time in social services and became a teacher in the International American School program and taught school in various places in the Middle East.

So what makes for war? Wars like World War I and II are pretty straight forward. We were defending ourselves and our allies against nations that were hell bent on destroying us; those wars were self-defence. Other wars are not nearly so straight forward, like Korea and Viet Nam, let alone those wars that are happening or are pending in the Middle East. The lines between self-defence and aggression become extremely blurred, cloudy and vague. I remember my then 90 year old father commenting that invading Iraq after 9-11 was sort of like if we had invaded Korea after Pearl Harbor.

Wars don't begin with armies and weapons. Wars end with armies and weapons and in the meantime countless people on all sides, and mostly in between die, are wounded, scarred for life either in body, heart, mind and soul or all of the above, and destruction of cities, towns, homes and farmland continue the suffering long after the war is over. Wars begin in the human heart when greed and arrogance and perverted religious or political ideologies plant the seeds of persecution, oppression and eventually outright aggression which grow and bloom into a full-fledged war and the aggressors and the defenders go at it with increasingly horrifying results, and even in conquest or truce the seeds of resentment are already sown. For a very long time my father refused to eat rice or Japanese food or buy Japanese products. That attitude has faded over time mostly out of necessity. In some parts of our own country it seems like the Civil War never ended.

Fred Buechner wrote that "Peace is not just the absence of war, but the presence of love.", and he is totally correct. The advent of love can prevent wars, but once the war is underway or has happened it is very difficult to inject love into the equation, and we seem to exist in a perpetual continuum of one war leading to another. What we need is some way to break the cycle and love is the only way that can happen. When Jesus told us to love our enemies he was dead serious and as idealistic as that sounds, it is the truth.

One has to ask the difficult question as to why our enemies hate us so much that they are willing to die to destroy us and sacrifice countless innocent lives in the process. It's irrational to the point of being insane, but at the heart of the matter our enemies have reasons that to them are rational and sane. The Germans were convinced that they were the Arian race and were better than anyone and everyone else which justified their conquest and genocide. The Japanese had a similar attitude problem. The Soviet Communists had the same attitude problem which spread into China, Korea and Viet Nam. The radical, fundamentalist Islamic militants believe that God tells them to destroy anyone who is not a Muslim, including Muslims of different sects who disagree with them, but the roots of that anger and hate run deeper than religion in the Middle East. The roots of their anger and hate stem from centuries of colonialism, imperialism and oppression in which the British Empire invaded, conquered and carved up their world imposing their religions and social customs on them and destroying them if they didn't play the game by their new rules. One wonders why those Saudi Arabian skyjackers did what they did. Why were they so angry at us? Saudi Arabia is one of the wealthiest nations on earth because we and other nations buy their oil. So they have one of the highest standards of living in the world. Most people don't even need a job. But in investing in their oil we imposed our standards of living on them and essentially enslaved them to our standards of living and destroyed their traditional life styles. Not all of them go militant about that but there is a tremendous amount of resentment over there and no matter what we do we cannot simply impose our value systems, our political systems and our life styles on them. No one has the right to do that to anyone else.

My friend who served in the American Schools in the Middle East shared with me a book entitled *Nonviolent Soldier of Islam* about a Pashtun leader during the days of British occupation. His name was Badshah Khan and he was very good friends with Mahatma Ghandi. The Pashtun was and is a group of tribes occupying what is now northern Pakistan and Afghanistan. Actually one of the more dastardly things the British did was create the artificial border between Afghanistan and Pakistan essentially dividing the Pashtun people and pitting them against each other. The Pashtun were and are noted for being fiercely militant and they gave the British a very hard time. So Badshah Khan and Mahatma Ghandi got together and as Ghandi was leading non violent protests in India Badshah Khan convinced the Pashtun to do the same. They lay down their arms, protested the British occupation completely non-violently, and the British essentially slaughtered them. Interestingly enough, and the reason this story is so seldom told, is that the young British officer who was in charge of that operation was named Winston Churchill. Our troops in that region are still fighting those seeds of war.

When we honor and give thanks to and for all the men and women who served, suffered and died in all of the conflicts, wars and rumors of wars that we have endured (and are enduring) we have to remember what they served, suffered and died for, and they served, suffered and died for peace. Yes, they served, suffered and died defending our nation and our way of life and the nations and ways of life of our allies, but the goal, the anticipated outcome would be peace. They served, suffered and died in memory of peace they once knew and in hope that such peace could be restored.

The only way we can break the cycles of war is to accept and adopt the peace of Christ within us and among us, and that peace is just another name for the love and grace of God. Peace beyond our understanding but by and in and with the love and grace of God is well within our reach. In memory of all who served, suffered and dies, let us devote and commit ourselves to the peace of Christ and the love and grace of God.

Prayers

Our ever living, ever loving God we pray for peace; peace which passes all our understandings; peace we remember and peace we yearn for. We pray for peace in our hearts, minds, bodies, and spirits where even in the face of conflict we can stand tall and secure in our faith in your love and grace. We pray for peace within and among all people, everywhere, praying that you will lead us all in the ways of peace. We pray that all hostilities and all the seeds of anger and hate will cease and in their place sow seeds of wellness, wholeness, happiness and security.

We pray for all who have volunteered to go in harm's way; may they be safe and well and may their missions be attainable. We pray in sincere thankfulness for all who have served, suffered and died to serve our nation and our allies, but as Christ teaches us we also pray for our enemies past and present that may find peace in you and help open the doors to peace among all people everywhere. Amen.

That All May Be One

The motto of the United Church of Christ is "That all may be one." and that's quite fitting given that the United Church of Christ was formed by the merger of the Evangelical and Reformed Church and the Congregational Church, one the few truly successful mergers of denominations in the recent past. It's not that easy to merge denominations for two primary reasons: first is the broad view of tradition and second is financial constraint due to designated giving. The UCC tried to merge with the Disciples of Christ denomination back in the eighties but so much money had been given either to the UCC or the Disciples with the stipulation that if their denomination ever ceased to be they wanted their money back. Despite the fact that our polities are very similar, it just wouldn't work; there wouldn't be enough money left behind to make it viable.

Tradition though is the biggest hindrance to the merger of denominations just as it is the biggest hindrance to the merger of congregations. In the small town of one Church I served there were two Congregational Churches, two Roman Catholic Churches, two Episcopal Churches, two Methodist Churches and a smattering of affiliated and independent Baptists Churches and a Jehovas Witness Kingdom Hall, each within a five minute drive of each other and each struggling mightily with maintaining their buildings and property and on a given Sunday everybody who worshipped anywhere could fit together into any one of the larger Churches. We got together on occasion to talk about all this and tried mightily to find some common ground on which we could begin to discuss even simply sharing our worship spaces so we didn't have to heat every building every Sunday. A common phrase was "You can close your Church and we would welcome you with open arms, but we're not going to close our Church and come to your Church even though we know you'd welcome us with open arms." Nothing ever got off the ground, and with all sincere respect the biggest obstacle was and is "This has been my family's

Church for generations and I'm not going anywhere else."; gotta respect that truth.

On the flip side of this issue was another Church I served that was literally the only Church in town and everybody of any denomination came there, even some of the more relaxed Roman Catholics. At one time there had been five Churches in town, but after the Civil war about seventy five percent of the population moved westward to find farming land that was not saturated with rocks and boulders, and then in the 1940's the entire center of town burned to the ground talking with it two Churches, one Church was sold and moved to a neighboring town, one was simply abandoned and later also burned to the ground, and another was dismantled and the materials were used to build other buildings. Given their very limited resources all they could do was to get together and build a meeting house about the size of this one and later build a Sunday school/day care/fellowship hall building, but was everybody's Church.

Given the history of this building being moved down the hill by teams of oxen, I often reflect on another town I lived in where at some time in the past they attempted to move their building down a hill to be close to the train station because they had visions of that area becoming the new center of town. Well, something went oops and the building got away from them and was absolutely destroyed, but there again they dismantled what was left of it and built new buildings with the remains. The old timers loved to point out, "See those windows? They came out of the Church. See that front door? That used to be one of the doors to the Church."; and on and on.

Despite the fact that we naturally maintain our historical traditions about where we worship and how we worship, there is the underlying assumption that we are all doing basically the same thing: worshiping God, learning about Christ's teachings and endeavoring, as a worshipping community, to put them to work in our lives, in our communities and in our larger world. I have long been interested and involved in ecumenical movements but though we clergy types can sit around together in our various vestments and talk about how we really are all one in Christ, there's really not that much to show for it. Unless one is totally immersed in and/or addicted to hard core, high-falutin' doctrine and dogma we have much more common ground than we do have differences. When it all boils down to brass tacks, we are all doing basically the same thing: worshiping God, learning about

Christ's teachings and endeavoring, as a worshipping community, to put them to work in our lives, in our communities and in our larger world.

We have to remember that Christ did not come to create a new religion or a new Church, and certainly not to create a Church that has fragmented into myriads of denominations and multitudes of different worshipping communities. His vision and his teachings are that all people everywhere are equally the beloved children of God. It is as simple yet profound as that. His message is offered equally and inclusively to all people. What it all comes down to, is that our religions, our doctrines and our dogmas and, to some extent our traditions tend to get in the way of that sense of oneness among all people. We focus too much on our differences rather than our common ground as beloved children of God, even to the point of sometimes having the audacity to claim that "We're beloved children of God, but they're not." That is totally contrary to Christ's essential message.

So we have all our differences between congregations, we have all our differences between our denominations. Some are simple and almost a moot point. Some are radical and complex, but we will all at least verbally affirm that somehow or other we are all one in Christ. When it comes to different religions the differences tend to be much more pronounced, radical and complex, but from our perspective, using our language we can affirm that we are all one in God, by whatever name we use for what we call God, we are each and all beloved children of our Creator; our God.

I believe that the differences between congregations and denominations will disappear over time, but it will probably happen more due to financial constraints which by forcing us to work together we will find more and more common ground. Many denominations are already consolidating their congregations as they simply cannot afford to keep so many Churches open. That is partly due to the fact that we are in the third generation of children who have no experience in the Church or in faith whatsoever, and unfortunately faith is extremely difficult to learn or attain to as an adult like taking an elective college course or something, all of which is to say that in general Church attendance is at an all time low. Some mega-Churches are thriving but most Churches are struggling in their own relative ways, some struggle to simply survive, and an increasing number of Church buildings stand vacant.

I also believe that the differences between religions will eventually evolve away, especially with the rapidly emerging global community where people of many nations and religions are working together side by side. The best way to get to know someone is by working together side by side and the best way to begin getting beyond our religious differences is by coming to understand each other and so learn to respect each other. Something profound might happen; we just might come to realize that we really all are beloved children of God.

We gather at this communion table to remember and celebrate our common-unity in Christ, in God, in the truth that we indeed are all one in God as beloved children of God. As a ritual this is a spiritual confession and a communal statement of faith that we believe, we know and we dedicate ourselves to the truth that in Christ; in God, we indeed all have been made as one and we all will become as one.

Prayers

Our God, all that exists comes from you: all things, all life, and all beings. We are one in that we have but one creator: You. The distances and barriers we set up between each other are artificial; our own creations. Help us understand that no one has an exclusive on you, but even as we have our differing understandings of you and perceptions of you there is still only one You.

Help us truly learn how to worship and so serve you, not our institutions, doctrines, dogmas and rituals, perceptions and understandings. Help us open up our spiritual senses and acknowledge that you are so much more than we can know, yet the constant remains that you are our Creator, not the other way around. You create us in your image and sometimes we try to create you in our image. Help us allow you to be the mystery that makes yourself know to us.

You present us with infinite, eternal and uncompromisable love and grace. Help us open ourselves the power of your presence and help us allow it to permeate our lives and so help us come to understand that we indeed one in and only in You.

Amen.

GOD IS STILL SPEAKING . . . ARE WE STILL LISTENING?

I remember back when I was in my later years of Sunday school, or perhaps during my Confirmation class, a thought dawned on me that has pretty much stuck with me throughout my life and has had a major influence on my life. I asked why it was that once upon a time, long ago and far away, during Bible times to be specific; why did God then talk to people face to face, why did God then make miracles happen right in that here and now, why did people write down all these things and called them scripture, but ever since then has God not said or done anything worthy of being written down as scripture? Why do we pay so much attention to what God said or did thousands of years ago? Hasn't God done anything new since then? Why did God stop doing new things worthy of being called scripture?

I don't remember exactly how my youth minister responded to that question, but by my not remembering an answer to that question from him that at least satisfied my curiosity at the time, I have to honestly say that I have never gotten a good answer to that question and I've been looking for an answer ever since. Why did God only speak to people face to face and make miracles happen in real time back then, but not ever since?

The stock answer comes from the presumed authority of Church doctrine. We, the Church, have a record of what God said and did way back then, the Church adopted that record as scripture, which cannot be added to or taken away from, and that's that: it is Church doctrine. Well rabble rousing me has never accepted that as a good answer to that question. It doesn't even address the question: why did God only speak to people face to face and make miracles happen in real time back then, but not ever since? That void in which that question remains unanswered leaves me feeling like everybody who has ever lived after this scriptural authority was established has been cheated out of something that could be really good and really exciting. Just imagine what it would be like if we were allowed to really believe and see and know that God is still speaking and doing miraculous things right here and now, all the time. Well, that's the point of this sermon if not the point to my whole ministry: God is still speaking and doing miraculous things right here and now all the time. The original question evolves into a new question: are we still listening to and are we still paying attention to God?

Unfortunately the notion that God only spoke and did miracles way back then, as recorded in the Bible, which is the perspective and attitude of many forms of Christian doctrine, isolates us from, if not shields us from the notion that we bear some responsibility for keeping our eyes and ears open to the fact that God is still speaking and doing miraculous things right here and now. It's much easier to say and believe that everything we need to know about God or to expect from God is already written down in the Bible so we don't need to keep looking for or anticipating anything new. It's much safer to hold up the Bible and say everything we need to know about God is right here in my hand. In light of that sense of Biblical authority, it's a bit risky and it's a bit scary to open ourselves to the possibility that we individually and collectively have some responsibility for keeping our eyes and ears open to what God might be saying and doing right here and now. What we find God saying and doing in the here and now might just challenge what we find in the Bible and the assumption that the Bible is the highest and final authority over what God is and is all about. There were times in history when I would have been burned at the stake for saying that.

I want to dig a little bit into what we call the authority of scripture. It all starts with the fact that for countless generation's people had no written language. Everything they remembered and everything they did was passed on orally; stories were passed on by oral tradition. You might remember in the TV series Roots the main character went back to Africa to find out what he could about his ancestor Kunta Kinte who was brought to America as a slave. He sat as an elder recited the tribe's history for hours on end until he finally came to Kunta Kinte and the main character found his roots. That's the way it was for all of humanity for thousands of years. The advent of written language changed all that as the oral traditions evolved into written traditions.

The problem was that very few people could read or write and those who could were revered as being extremely special persons. The Scribes of the Old Testament were as revered as the Priests, if not more so, because not many of the Priests could read or write themselves. Imagine how miraculous it would have been to be in the presence of a person who could pick up a manuscript like a scroll and look at these funny little scribbles and make sense of them and read them to you. That person had some special power! In most cases the Scribes were chosen as youth and hidden away in enclaves or monasteries where they were taught to read and write. Reading and writing were sacred and secret. One had to attain to the power of being able to read and write and in the process what was written and read aloud was given the highest respect and took on the highest authority.

It is generally agreed that written languages evolved into being in about 3500 BC at least in our ancestral Mesopotamian region. Egyptian hieroglyphics evolved in their own direction and Cuneiform evolved into our own ancestral languages. People had to wait until 1450 AD for the written language to become available to the common people via Gutenberg's printing press. For almost 5000 years the written language was hand written and its availability was limited to the rich, the powerful and most exclusively to the clergy of the Church. The Bible took on its authority firstly because it simply was a written document, and any and all written documents were held in very high regard, and that sacredness and high authority was signed, sealed and delivered by the sacredness and sanctity of those who could read it.

In 397 AD a council of Christians in Carthage established what we now refer to as the Old Testament, the Apocrypha and the New Testament, ending roughly three hundred years of controversy and haggling over which books and letters were to be considered sacred texts. Scholars argue over why certain books and letters were kept or eliminated but no one since that council of 397 AD has been able to change what we now call the Bible. Of course, as I have expounded upon at length if not ad nauseum, the act of translating the Bible from the original Hebrew and Greek has brought about many changes in the context of the Bible, but not the order of the books and letters. The discovery of many other books and letters which were not adopted by the Council at Carthage has opened the debate about what is or should be considered sacred texts but as of today nobody has dared challenge the authority of what we now call the Bible except a few rabble rousers like me, and I actually do not challenge the authority of the Bible but I do join ranks with the many who challenge how it is translated, interpreted and used to justify things that the Bible never intended. Believe it or not, there was considerable opposition by the Church to Gutenberg publishing the Bible and allowing it to fall into the hands of the common people who just might catch on to the shenanigans the Church was getting away with by their interpretations of the Bible and it's authority. I guess I caught on. Knowledge is a good thing.

Last week I talked about the original motto of the United Church of Christ which is "That all may be one." A few years back the UCC adopted another motto which is "God is still speaking," which I take great delight in because it seems that at last someone is trying to openly answer the question I had carried around all my life. No, God did not stop speaking when the Council at Carthage sealed the Bible in sacred sanctity and authority. No, God did not stop performing miracles after raising Jesus from the dead.

The Bible is basically a record of God's interactions with people; God's conversations with people. There was nothing special about those people as if God chose to talk to them alone and nobody else. What is recorded as literal word for word conversations are most certainly embellishment, enhancement and just plain good folk tale talk, but this doesn't mean they are not true. I probably would not say that God told me to go to seminary and become a minister, but at the same time that is essentially what happened. It wasn't a voice booming out of thunderhead or a phone call from George Burns, but when we talk about being told by God or being called by God we are, in our faith, saying that God talks to us.

When we talk about God speaking to us in the here and now we are talking about speaking and listening through our faith; a different sense of speech and a different sense of hearing that is as readily available to us as it was to the characters in the Bible. Closing the cover of the Bible as the highest authority on God closes the door on our having our own personal relationships with God, which is what the Good News is really all about: not just what happened long ago and far away, but what is and can be happening right now.

So show me a miracle that God is performing right now. The first miracle is that we are here at all and add to that that we have such amazing bodies, hearts, minds and spirits to be alive in. Just because science can explain things in scientific language doesn't mean that what is and what is happening is not miraculous. I have no quarrel with the notion that it has taken what appears to be about 16 billion years to create the present cosmos. Six days is a poetic metaphor, but it's saying the same thing: God creates the cosmos. To hear God speaking and see God's miracles we have to open our whole beings to the power of the presence of God and know that it is as real as the air we breathe and when we do that something really good and really exciting is sure to happen.

Prayers

Our God speak to us in this here and now. We about of your wondrous and miraculous presence in people thousands of years ago, but are you still doing wondrous and miraculous things today? Some of our traditions would have it that you are aloof and watching us from a distance. Why would it seem that you once were so present and now you are so far away? Break the silence, shatter the stillness, roar like thunder, fly like the wind and make the power of your presence known to us right here and now. Let us be the ones who can truly say that you have talked to us, you have shown us wondrous things; you are making miracles happen. You call each and every one of to be priests and scribes, prophets and apostles and what you can do in our lives is just as important as what you did in others lives centuries even millennia ago. Help us wake up to your presence right here and now and hear you speak and see you act as you call us to be witnesses to your presence and teachers of your loving truth. Help us no longer hide behind the illusion that everything that you have done is already done and embolden us to see and believe and live the truth that every day, every instant you are constantly making all things new.

We could use some newness in our lives God: where we are broken help us be made whole, where we are ill or injured help us be healed, where our relationships are strained help us embrace each other in your love.

Amen.

In the Eye of the Beholder

Some say you can't teach and old dog new tricks. Well, I'm not such an old dog and I greatly enjoy learning new tricks, new things, new perspectives and new ideas. I think I got this from my grandmother because up until her dying day she was always inquisitive; she always wanted to hear something new; she took great delight in any bit of new knowledge and experience.

I was listening to Science Friday on WNPR (2:00 every Friday afternoon) and I learned something new that I had never imagined and it has set my speculative and creative juices flowing. It's a touch complicated, but I'll do my best to explain it. The human eye contains thousands of sets of arrays that sense light. The basic sensors perceive black and white and shades of grey. Many other sets of sensors basically see in three colors: red, yellow and blue. Our brains take those perceptions of red, yellow and blue and combine them. Red and yellow become orange, blue and yellow become green, red and blue become purple and so we see in a rainbow, for example, the classic red, orange, yellow, green, blue and purple and all the various shades in between. So that's how the human eye works: the sensors see basically three colors and the brain expands that into six colors and all the shades in between.

We probably all knew that but what I never knew nor imagined is that other creature's eyes have very different arrangements and collections of sensors. Some have less than three basic sensors, but others have many more, which means that they see in many colors than we do. The common dragon fly sets the record with sixteen sensors, so a dragon fly sees 16 basic colors and their brains combine them into at least 32 colors and all the shades in between. Just imagine that: being able to see in 32 colors and the multitudes of shades in between! We can't really imagine that because we can't see like that and our imaginations can only go as far as our senses go.

When you look at the total array of radiations that exist in our universe, laid out in a long spectrum, in the center is the little array we call visible light: the rainbow. Everything else is invisible to us. We have created instruments that can "see" some of those other radiations and translate them into colors that we can see, but we can see only in the six basic colors our eyes and brains are attuned to. The miraculous fact, that is news to me, remains that other creatures can "see" in many more colors than we can. Scientists had long speculated that other creatures can see maybe not as many colors as we do or the same colors to different degrees. Deer, for example are assumed to not be able to see bright orange so wearing bright orange in the woods during hunting season is, at the same time, good camouflage and good insurance that another hunter won't shoot you. Some animals can see much better in low light than we can and some have much sharper vision that can see a mouse in the brush from 500 feet in the air. It is speculated that migratory birds and other animals can see the earth's magnetic field or the ultraviolet reflections of water in the air. We don't know exactly what this all means because we cannot get into their brains and see what they see, and even if we could we could only see what our brains can see, limited by the sharpness of our lenses. To go to the extreme on this path, it is quite possible that what I see as red, orange, yellow, green, blue and purple may not be what you see as red, orange, yellow, green, blue and purple, or what other creatures see as red, orange, yellow, green, blue and purple, whatever that means from their perspective.

"OK Carl, so where are you going with all this? I didn't come here to hear a science lecture. What's all this got to do with God?" Well, to me it's got everything to do with God because I am always glad to be reminded that one of the most important aspects about God, our Creator, is that God is a great mystery. There is so much that we do not and cannot know about God from our fledgling human perspectives, and I am personally very skeptical about people, institutions and other—osophies and—ologies that assume they have got God all figured out. This is not a criticism so much as it is an obvious fact of reality. In a world polarized by love and hate, good and evil and all the human suffering that goes with it, I am comforted in knowing there is much more to all this than meets the eye (pun intended). Like invisible, unimaginable colors, God is so much more than we can or see even imagine.

The process of coming to allow God to be the mystery that God is can be very disconcerting and even threatening to some people, but it shouldn't be and needn't be. By allowing God to be the mystery that God is there is always room for more, there is always the adventure of finding out more about God and there is always the real possibility that God is trying to reveal God's self to us in ways we might not be able to see or imagine right now. Allowing God to remain a mystery allows us to allow ourselves to keep our hearts and minds and whole beings open to the infinite possibilities of God; the ultimate "What If?" that keeps our creative juices flowing, our minds wondering and our dreams dreaming. Allowing God to be a mystery is our greatest source of hope in a world that needs all the hope it can get.

So where do we find this hope as we move into a mostly uncharted and unknown future? We get hope for the future by looking at promises and hopes fulfilled in the past. It's not just through human events that we can find hope. In fact just looking at human events can be very myopic and limited in the scope of finding hope. We have to look way back towards, if not to, the beginning which is actually impossible to imagine because we cannot conceive of infinity in a finite world, nor can we conceive of eternity in a world so completely governed by beginnings and endings. But as far back as we can look what do we see? We see God at work. We see God creating and we see God sustaining. Again, whether it took six days or sixteen billion years we see the same thing: God creating then, now and always. The evolution of time, space, matter and energy; the advent and evolution of all life into the most amazing things we are today, as all of God's creatures, is God's handiwork and it is by no means a done deal; it's not over; it's not ever over. There is always something new happening; something to anticipate; something to hope for. Seeing the faithfulness of God all the way down through history is to find the trust and confidence that the future will be something that God will see as being is "Very good" just as God ". . . saw that it was very good." back in the beginning (whenever, however that was).

The biggest trick and the most important thing in the whole process is to be very mindful that God is indeed a mystery and not to assume that our perceptions sum up the whole of the reality that is God. Trying to imagine what it would be like see in multitudes of colors that we honestly can't imagine is a good dose of humble pie. We are reminded of our limitations which is a good antidote to our tendencies towards arrogance. But at the same time that we are reminded of our limitations we are also reminded of the infinite and eternal possibilities of God.

The scientists who endeavor to unlock the mysteries of how our eyes work, how our bodies work in all their meticulous, miraculous ways, how our minds work, how creation in general works, are not defining God. They are simply coming to understand God's handiwork, and by understanding it hopefully come up with cures for maladies and diseases and crises that were once thought to be utterly impossible to do anything about. The evolution of our scientific understandings of creation and all things in it is not a challenge to God; it's not an affront to God; it's an ongoing, living example of God's creativity working in and through us. It's a sign of hope that we can come to know more, do more, understand more and by doing so enhance of understandings of and our relations within and among each and all creatures within God's creation.

Well within our memories of our own human history we have seen ourselves attain to the potential to live longer, healthier, happier lives. We have grown bigger, stronger and smarter in many ways, though we still tend to carry around backpacks full of arrogance, indifference and prejudices. Hopefully one day we will evolve as a global community into a world in which we will have put aside all the artificial barriers between us and by whatever names and languages we use we will all know that we indeed God's beloved children and treat each other as such.

Prayers

Our God, please surprise us, show us something new. Even more so, help us open our eyes, our hearts and minds, all our senses to the truth that indeed you are continuously doing something new; creating something new, moving creation along on its next steps in your eternal and infinite evolution of your creation.

We can remember some of the past and we can prophecy some of the future, but we are here and now and this here and now is all we have. From this vantage point we see in the mirror dimly, but the time will come, you assure us, when we see you face to face; now we only understand in part, but the time will come, you assure us, when we will understand as completely as we have been understood. Help that truth; help that hope truly be the keel and rudder of the ship of our faith. Though we don't see or understand it all, help our faith in your creativity keep us on a straight course towards the fulfillment of your creation, the establishment of your kingdom. Amen.

SACRAMENT

A sacrament is a sacred moment; a moment in time and space in which we recognize, honor and celebrate that something sacred has happened or is happening in or among persons. Most every ritual we go through in the Church has its roots in something sacred. Most everything we do in life can be seen as having its roots in something sacred.

The Catholic Church recognizes seven sacraments: Baptism, Confirmation, Holy Communion, Confession, Marriage, Ordination, Anointing the Sick and Last Rites. The early Protestants, primarily Martin Luther and John Calvin, decided that was too many so they cut the sacraments down to two: Baptism and Holy Communion. Their reasoning was that a true sacrament had to be something that Jesus himself had done. Jesus never confirmed anyone, never took confession, never married anyone, never ordained anyone, never anointed anyone nor said last rites over anyone, though for many some of these claims were and are debatable. It was not a simple debate; it was very contentious and it pitted the Roman Catholic Church against the Protestants and in some cases pitted Protestants against Protestants. It really was the issue of the sacraments that split the Church asunder.

To boil it all down to a simple nutshell, a sacrament, in our tradition is an outward and visible sign of something happening within a person or persons that we believe is sacred. God is doing something, not us. In children's baptism we celebrate the new person as a gift of God's grace to that child in their self as well as to all the rest of us who will share the child's life. The Roman Church believes that an infant must be baptized as soon as possible after birth because if the child died without being baptized they would not share in God's love and grace in heaven. A morbid thought to be sure. Baptism can also be used as a sign and symbol of forgiveness and cleansing. Baptists believe only in that form of baptism, believing that salvation is attained only through grace; a free gift of God and no ritual is necessary for that. They baptize people when they are about 12 or 13 because they believe that by that age the person will know and understand that they need to be forgiven and cleansed. Many people of many traditions, our own included, will baptize people at any age as they feel the need for forgiveness and cleansing.

The point, from our Protestant perspective, is that the ritual of the sacrament does not make something happen that wasn't already happening in and by the love and grace of God. It's not magic. In children's baptism we celebrate that God has already blessed the child by creating her or him. In adult baptism is already forgiven and blessed and we celebrate that with them. It's all God's doing, not ours. In a marriage we celebrate and give thanks for the love the two people have found together and enlivened in their relationship. *We* don't marry them, God does and we celebrate that. The only real thing that a clergy person or JP does is sign the license making it all legal. I often reflect on how simple it is for me to sign a piece of paper; I don't even have to perform a ceremony to make it legal, but then comes all the craziness it takes to undo what I signed, and I am not in any way included in the process of un-signing anything. I believe that the Church abdicated it's authority over marriage by allowing marriage to become a strictly legal issue; another topic for another time.

Our other sacrament, the Lord's Supper, is treated the same way. The key words for us are "Do this in remembrance of me." Unlike in the Catholic Church where it is believed that the priest magically transforms the bread into Jesus' actual body and the wine into Jesus' actually blood; we simply share the bread and grape juice in remembrance of Jesus' being with us. Jesus certainly used the bread and wine symbolically; so do we. I like adding the words, "He wasn't going to have a body anymore, so he calls to be his body. He wasn't going to have any life blood anymore so he calls to be his life blood." I think that is what he meant by sharing the bread and cup with his disciples, and we are all his disciples. The Roman and other orthodox Churches also believe that the Eucharist, as they call it, is in fact the Medicine of Immortality and without regular doses of it you're not going to get into heaven. Denying a person the Eucharist was/is seen as essentially sending the person to hell. The Last Rites are intended to offset the possibility that the person had not received the Eucharist soon enough before they died.

We do not view ordination as a formal sacrament but ordination certainly is sacramental; we are celebrating something that God has done and is doing. When someone is ordained, *we* don't ordain them; we celebrate the fact that God ordains them by calling them into the ministry and in ordination we affirm that they are adequately prepared to do so. I certainly will never forget getting down on my knees in the front of the First Church of Christ, Congregational in Farmington and having dozens and dozens of hands laid on me as the presiding Clergy proclaimed and prayed me ordained. That wasn't all about me; it was all about the love, grace and calling of God. When I stood up I wouldn't have been surprised to see burn marks in the carpet. I have felt the same way about every other ordination I have participated in. It's a classic example of "Let go and let God!" God's making all this happen, not us.

One thing I admire about my Buddhist friends is how they have such a different perspective on what is sacred and sacramental. Simply put, a classic Buddhist sees all things as being sacred and all actions as being sacramental. There really is no reason that we couldn't all take on that same perspective. Creation is God's creation, so it can be seen as sacred. The simple act of enjoying the beauty of God's sacred creation can be seen as a sacrament: a sacred moment. The simple act of eating the fruit of God's creation, which gives and sustains our lives, can be seen as a sacrament; a sacred moment. Breathing the air of God's creation that gives and sustains our lives can be seen as a sacrament; a sacred moment. Listening to the rhythms of our hearts pumping our life blood through our bodies is listening to a sacred rhythm. There are so many sacred things we do and participate in every day, every moment.

Being aware of the sacred and the sacramental creation we are and are an integral part of is what the Buddhists call being mindful. We tend not to be mindful of what we are experiencing or doing at any given time. We take a snap shot of a beautiful sunset as if we could capture it on film. Nothing can capture the full experience of a sunset: it is a process, it changes, it takes time, it comes and it goes it involves the smell of the rain, the feeling of the rain on our faces, the breeze on our skin. The full experience of a sunset is what is sacred, not just the moment we capture of a sunset, even though as it is with a ritual, the experience of looking at the snapshot can remind us of the whole experience. A ritual should remind us of an experience that is much bigger than the ritual itself

We tend to just gobble up our food without thinking about where it came from. Sometimes we'd maybe rather not like to know where it came from, though we certainly should, but the fact of the matter remains that if our food is actually going to feed us in a healthy, wholesome way it must come from the creation that gives and sustains our lives. If we were more mindful of that we'd all have many fewer health issues. The same holds true for breathing issues, smoking and pollution included.

Being mindful of the sacredness, the sacramental reality of being and living; being mindful of everything we are and everything we are a part of is or should be like praying. I've probably shared the story before, but I learned more about praying from my Buddhist friends than anywhere else. They challenged me by saying that we tend to pray as if we're offering a shopping list to God. In some ways we do and that is good, but the other side of praying for a Buddhist is quite simply to shut up and listen; to quiet one's mind, to turn off the background noise, to engage the silence and listen and hear the still small voice of God.

So what can we expect to hear when we shut up and open our whole selves to the still, small voice of God? Ultimately there is no such thing as total silence. We can discipline ourselves to quiet down all our inner conversations, to stop or at least shut out all external noises. But what we are left with are the sounds of our breathing, the beating of our hearts, the myriad of physical sensations that our bodies feel all the time, and when we are left with that we can find that we are listening to the essential sounds of being and being alive which is sacred and sacramental, and in that mindfulness we can know that we are hearing the still small voice of God telling us "You are alive, you are my child and I love you." What more could we wish to hear?

Prayers

Creator God, ever living, ever loving God, you instill your sacredness into everything you create, from the tiniest particle to the total infinite and eternal scope of the cosmos, and every thing, every being; all that exists and has life and you say that it is all good; it is all blessed. We acknowledge and confess that there are times and events in which your sacredness seems to be overwhelmed by the evil we create for ourselves and each other, but these times and events are the exception, not the norm, and by your grace and love you would and can turn anything evil into your loving good.

Help us see, hear, smell, touch and know that all you create is sacred and everything we do can be sacramental, if it is not already. Help us be mindful of what we are experiencing, what we are doing that we can see the sacredness that comes to us, creates and supports us, and know that by our thoughts, words and deeds we can make sacred things happen also.

We thank you for all the blessings that come our way every day, and help us be mindful of them so we can share them with each other. Amen.

WHO WE CAN BE

The day inevitably comes, in the life of every parent, when the question of "What do you want to be when you grow up?" is asked of your child either by you or someone else. What usually happens is that the assumption is made that the child somehow needs to know they want to be when they grow up at an early age long before they have adequate life experience to answer that question. The usual response from the child is confusion, though in their wonderful innocence they can make a game out of it. My first image of what I wanted to be when I grew up was that I wanted to an engineer; not someone who designs buildings and machinery but someone who drives a train. A visit to the Peabody Museum in New Haven led me up the path of wanting to be paleontologist. By the time I was set down in a guidance counselor's office as a freshman in high school to make a formal decision about where my high school career would be heading and thus where my college career would lead me, I honestly had no idea what I wanted to be when I grew up but I **HAD** to choose something, so I just blurted out, "Well, I might be interested in engineering." denying my first dream of wanting to drive a train in favor of designing buildings and machinery. I honestly don't know where that answer came from, but as I said, I **HAD** to say something. I had absolutely no idea what I wanted be when I grew up, I honestly had no interest in engineering (though I would still like to drive a train someday) but I **HAD** to say something.

A year or so later I went through what I consider to be my most life changing moment. I had always been active in my Church, I deeply admired my ministers and was very interested in the life of our faith, and it suddenly dawned on me, literally in the middle of the night that I wanted to be a minister when I grew up. It was a clear as a bell, no doubt about it experience and I have never had any doubts or regrets about my life's calling. I went in and made my announcement to the guidance counselor who looked at me with a dumb, blank look on his face and stammered out something like "Well . . . er . . . um . . . there's nothing we offer in high school to help prepare for that . . . so . . . you might as well just take the standard courses, but and you may be interested in our senior year Humanities class when you get there." I smiled and walked out of the room thinking "Gotcha!" As a senior I was accepted into the Humanities class and it's the only high school course I remember at all.

When my daughters started asking questions about what they wanted to be when they grew up I told them "Don't be in any great hurry. The time will come when you will know. Take your time; explore different subjects and interests and experiences. Look at me, I'm thirty something, and I still don't know what I want to be when I grow up." "But you're a minister Dad and you are grown up.' they would inevitably fire back. I would laugh and tell them "Yep, I'm a minister, but that's not all I am: I'm a woodworker, carpenter, photographer, poet, gardener and lots more, and when you 'grow up' and have a career or a job that won't be all you are either, so don't let anyone push you into making a decision **RIGHT NOW.** They each explored, experienced and floundered around for a while. My eldest excelled in math, finishing college calculus while still in high school and thought about teaching, but ended up with a graduate degree in Sports Management and now runs all the special sports programs at UCONN. My middle daughter was very interested in teaching but ended up as a licensed Massage Therapist, but put all that aside to raise her two daughters at home with her veterinarian husband. My youngest was very interested in Environmental Issues but ended up with a Dean's List degree in Art and now designs and makes jewelry.

Somebody once said that if you really enjoy what you're doing you'll never work a day in your life. Maybe once upon a time one could set one goal for one's life and live it out successfully and happily. Once upon a time most people were farmers and usually had one or more other skills, like carpentry or blacksmithing or something. The industrial revolution changed all that. Now one had a full time job and whatever else they had time to do was more of a hobby than work. Today fewer and fewer people end up with one lifetime career. That's due to variables in the economy plus the fact that we tend to be overwhelmed with information about options: there are lots of open doors out there. I took a sabbatical from the Parish ministry and took up the ministry of teaching people how to build houses for people in need with Habitat for Humanity, but the center of my heart remains firmly committed to ministry in many forms and I still turn wood, make photographs, build stuff and occasionally write a poem. I like the phrase "Be all you can be." but I never served in the military.

God invites us to be all we can be too. Christ offers us a living example of all we can be, but in many ways all we can be tends to be well beyond even our imaginations. There are lots of things that can hold us back from being all we can be in God's vision of who we can be and many of these hindrances originate in the doctrines and dogmas we have adopted as the roots of our faith, and often the very faith that should set us free and empower and enable us to be all we can be limits us, hinders us and traps us.

We can be seriously hindered by guilt, but one of the key truths about God and Christ is that we are forgiven. When we ask for forgiveness and accept forgiveness we are set free from the past and a brand new future opens up for us. We can be seriously hindered by doubt, but if we believe and take seriously Jesus' teachings that God is the truth and God's truth will set us free, we are indeed set free. We can be seriously hindered by feelings of inadequacy, but we are taught that God accepts us just as we are and whatever we can do with and for God is more than enough. We can be seriously hindered by self doubts and self loathing, but we are also taught that the bottom line in God's relationship with creation, including us is that God loves us unconditionally.

On the flip side we can be seriously hindered in being all we can be by arrogance and pride. The Psalmist says ". . . walk humbly with your God . . ." God is God and we're not and though in the eyes of God we are all God's beloved children, that doesn't mean that any one of us is more important or more blessed than anyone else. We can be seriously hindered by ignorance, which includes prejudice and not allowing the mystery that is God to be the mystery that God is. We will never have God all figured out and every time we open a new door in science or knowledge in general or even God, many new doors appear awaiting to be opened.

Being all we can be is not a onetime goal that we can attain to and then it's all over; we've arrived, we're here, we're there. Becoming all we can be is an ongoing, lifelong process, and in the great mystery that is God, it is a process that goes well beyond what we now know as life. The cosmos is constantly evolving. We are constantly evolving. The only things that are constant are faith, hope and love: God's faith in us and our faith in God, our hope in God and God's hope for us, and God's unconditional, ever present, eternal and infinite, unceasing and unchanging love for each and every one and all of us.

Prayers

Our God, open up our hearts and minds and remind us that there is so much we can be, we can do, we can dare and we can dream that so often get lost in the seemingly overwhelming complexities of life and the dull and boring routines of life. Re mind us that you offer us the total vastness of the cosmos: everything, every creature, every experience and you invite us to explore and delve into the wonders and mysteries that surround us and live within us.

Help us truly be all we can be, knowing that in your infinite possibilities nothing is impossible to you. Even as we embrace your love and grace in our faith, help us remain open to infinite and eternal mystery that you are allowing room for new experiences, new knowledge, new experiences of your love and grace in any and all aspects of our lives alone and together. Following Christ's ever-living example help us truly become and be your living body and your life blood, bringing your love and grace to life in all the ways our lives touch each other's lives.

It's hot; God and the heat can get us down. Life's not always as easy as we'd like it to be, and that can get us down. The physical, emotional, mental and spiritual stresses we live with can get us down. Pick us up God and help us all be whole, healthy and happy in your love and grace.

In silence we offer up our own personal prayers . . . waiting to hear your still, small voice . . .

Amen.

Prophecy

I started musing on this sermon Thursday afternoon when our thermometer, which sits directly in the sun on the back deck, maxed out at 120 degrees and the air felt like I needed scuba gear just to breathe. Even though I used to do construction work outside all day in weather like that I have to admit that I have lost much of my resiliency and I tend to get somewhat cranky about the heat and humidity these days. What kept me going was the weather forecast that the heat and humidity would break on Saturday and Sunday, today, would be much cooler and dryer. I had to trust that prophecy and it didn't let me down.

Prophecy is a big part of the Bible story and it is a big part of our faith. Contrary to the notion that prophecy is like magically envisioning an otherwise unknowable future like gazing into a crystal ball or reading tea leaves, prophecy is much more down to earth and practical. It is recognizing the causes and effects of what is happening right in the here and now. It is the wisdom of learning from the past and projecting that wisdom into the future. Prophecy is similar to weather forecasting in that one looks at all the available data about what one can expect to happen, based on what has happened or is happening. The difference between prophecy and weather forecasting is that prophecy adds in a significant factor of just plain faith that there are forces at work in our world that are much bigger and more powerful than just scientific data. Prophecy comes from recognizing that beyond the causes and effects of the past and present is a reality that is shaping the future even as we speak. We know that reality as God.

Prophecy is seeing what's happening right now, comparing it to the past and projecting it into the future. The effect of injustice is more injustice. The effect of violence is more violence. The effect of the widening void between those who have more than one could ever need and those who don't have enough to survive is increasing resentment, unrest, anger and violence. The effect of ignorance is more ignorance.

The effect of greed is more greed. The effect of hate is more hate, and the list goes on and on. These are all very human concerns and controversies and whatever the original causes were or are the effects continue snowballing sliding down an ever more slippery slope.

Some people like to talk about God's judgment as the center of this whole issue as if God punishes those who don't do God's will or do something contrary to God's will. If that was true then why do terrible things happen to otherwise perfectly good people and why do terrible people keep on doing terrible things? God doesn't toss around lightning bolts or make earthquakes, tornadoes, hurricanes and tsunamis happen as some kind of a judgment; a punishment, nor does God stand in judgment issuing threats. God doesn't make bad things happen; people make bad things happen and put themselves in harm's way. God wants only good things to happen. The problem is that we each and all bear the responsibility to make good things happen and stop bad things from happening. It's all up to us. God makes it perfectly clear what God wants to have happen and God gives us the free will within which to choose whether we will make good or bad things happen.

The really good news is that despite whatever choices we make God will never give up on us. The sobering reality of that good news is that God will not miraculously intervene when we blow it. Nations and civilizations have come and gone all the way down through history and it is a very dangerous assumption to make that we might somehow be exempt from that pattern. It is also a very dangerous assumption to assume that God is on our side, right or wrong, so whatever we do must be right with God. God may not intervene in human affairs directly to the extent that we might wish for but God will stand back and let us do unto ourselves and each other whatever we like, whether or not if we consider the truth of the Golden Rule that we should do unto others as we would like them to do unto us.

All of this is so totally down to earth. When people make bad things happen, or allow bad things to happen, bad things happen. When people make good things happen, and throw their support into those good things, good things happen. Prophecy is simply recognizing that truth and putting it to work in our lives.

The situation of global warming is a good case in point. Some people vehemently deny that any warming is going on at all. Some people say it is simply a natural effect of climate change. Some people say it's the entire fault of our pollution and carbon emissions. Some people couple climate change with our carbon emissions, but even the hardest hearted skeptics cannot deny that the polar ice and major glaciers are melting at an accelerating rate which means the earth's atmosphere and oceans are getting warmer and big changes are in looming on the horizon. Sea levels are rising, weather patterns are changing, formerly dry places are getting wet, formerly wet places are getting dry, cold places are getting warmer and warm places are getting colder, and on and on. I personally side with those who see this warming as partly a natural climate change but the fact is that our pollution and carbon emissions have been and are accelerating the whole effect. The fact is that even if we could miraculously, instantaneously stop emitting any pollution and carbon into the atmosphere and oceans at all, the cycle of warming is underway and we cannot immediately stop or reverse it. So what can we do about it? I prophecy that we had better start making preparations for these major changes and do everything we can to reduce if not eliminate our carbon footprints.

Climate change is nothing new. It's been going on for billions of years: cool down, warm up, freeze up and thaw out, the earth's crust rises and sinks. A few thousand years ago there was a mile of ice on top of us right here. A few billion years ago the Appalachian Mountain Range, including the White Mountains, was bigger and higher than the present day Himalayas. Mount Washington was at least as big and high as Mount Everest. Limestone found at the top of thousands of feet tall mountains was once at the bottom of a primordial sea. Closer to home, we human beings would not inhabit the entire planet if it had not been for the last couple of ice ages when the sea levels dropped to the point that we could walk from land mass to land mass. Sailing across oceans is a relatively new human invention.

One observation about human history that I like to ponder is that the story of the Garden of Eden is most likely based on real history. The vast deserts of the Sahara and places like it were once lush, fertile and abundant with life, including human beings. Penetrating radar shows river beds and settlements buried deep under the sand. Over time the deserts started taking over the garden until it was all but gone. Even within Biblical times where they talk about the Promised Land flowing with milk and honey; being incredibly fertile and abundant with life, now it eludes me how people can eke out a living from that semi arid land. Climate changes, and the biggest reason we human beings have survived these changes is that we are adaptable. So I prophesy that we'd better get adapting because, whether we like it or not, changes are on the way and they are starting to happen.

The consequences are huge and the changes needed are huge. The changes to our economy alone are mind blowing, as are the social and political ramifications, because we can't go on basing our economy and our standards of living on the cost of harming, if not destroying our environment, and as a population mass we are rapidly approaching the critical mass wherein we could do so. We only have one planet; one environment. I am acutely aware that I am child of the very real threat of mutually assured destruction during the fifties and sixties in the threat of thermonuclear war. I was forced to imagine a lifeless planet. I'd rather not dwell on that image, but to concern myself with helping to make sure it doesn't happen by any cause or for any reason.

The good news remains that God will never give up on us, and though God may not intervene directly into our practical human affairs, either good or bad, God keeps us going and God keeps on trying to show us the way: God's way. God's way is steadfast love. God's way is grace in the face of fear and guilt. God's way is forgiveness in the face of whether or not someone deserves forgiveness. God's way is compassion. God's way is keeping creation creating, moving ever forward towards the day when all of God's critters will live whole, healthy and happy lives. God's way is life over death, faith over doubt, truth over lies and light over darkness.

God keeps calling us, offering us, showing us that the way of life and wholeness and goodness is right in front of us; the Kingdom of God is at hand. All we have to do is reach out and take it and make it happen starting right here in our own lives, in our own families, in our own communities. We must be able and willing to embrace the reality that our world is changing not just climatically but a global community is beginning to emerge. We've got to tear down our artificial walls and let people come together. It's not going to be easy, but, God willing, it will happen, and God is more than willing to help us make it happen.

In the meantime we will plod along like Martin Bell's Rag Tag Army, moving only as fast as the slowest members, and God will wait patiently while we stop to smell a flower or catch a frog, or carry on one of our mindless, senseless wars. God will take care of those who others can't or won't take care of. God's never going to give up on us.

God's never going to stop loving each and every one of us, but the Kingdom of God, as close as it is, won't come to fulfillment until we do the same.

Prayers

Our God of all time and space, help us learn from the past, be mindful of what's happening right now and envision a future in which your love and grace are fulfilled and all people will live in peace having everything they need to live whole, healthy and happy lives. Yes, we may sometimes be dreamers but we only dream of what you have promised us. Help us live into your dream and make it real.

Your dream is so simple and obvious: all people want to be loved and to love in return. That is what the good life is really all about. We build barricades of petty misunderstandings based on our limited vision of what is good and evil, right and wrong. So many of these misunderstandings are couched in our social, political and even our religious institutions. That which should bring all people together in love and peace and wellbeing becomes the obstacles to that happening. Wake us up, break us open, help us prophecy your promises, your future, your love and grace.

We are bombarded with bad news from every direction: wars and rumors of wars, prejudice anger and hate abound, natural disasters and totally unnatural disasters, horrific crimes and horrific injustice. Like a heat wave all this bad news tends to chew away at us; at our hope, our inner peace, even our faith. Bring us back to life in the cool, clear, refreshing wonders of your love knowing that all this shall pass and your day is coming. Amen.

KING OF THE JEWS

We tend to not make much of the fact that Jesus was a Jew. He was born, raised, and educated as a Jew. Though his father was a carpenter, a trade that he would have learned, his life career, though short lived was that of a teacher; a Rabbi. It is unlikely that he could read or write; that distinction was given to the few elite among the scribes, Pharisees and Sadducees. Back then, as it is in many places in our world today, scripture and its teachings were memorized and passed on orally.

In his time the Sadducees were made up of the priestly, aristocratic class and they held rule over the practices of the people's faith and the goings on in the temple. The Pharisees pretty much took care of the more mundane, secular issues. The Romans, at the time, were really quite tolerant of local religions and governments, but held the local authorities responsible for making sure that Roman taxes got collected and passed on to the Romans and also held them responsible for settling any unrest among the people towards the Romans. It was a dire day if the Romans had to intervene in a local rebellion. They were, quite simply, quite brutal. Jesus was born into a time when the usually cordial relations between the Jews and the Romans were beginning to sour.

It is not clear exactly if Jesus sided with either the pro-Romans or the con-Romans. One of the things that got Jesus dragged before the Sadducees and Pharisees was the accusation that he was claiming that he had more authority over the people than the Romans did, which, in actuality was not the case as he did claim he had more authority over the people and their faith than the Sadducees and Pharisees did. He pointedly challenged their interpretations of scripture and their doctrinal and dogmatic policies and practices. The Sadducees and Pharisees knew that they couldn't shut Jesus up because he was very popular with the people, so they trumped up charges for which the Romans could shut him up. Pilate asked Jesus, "Are you the King of the Jews?" If he had said yes, he would have been denying the truth that the Jews hadn't had a King for ages, and it wouldn't have mattered to the Romans because they would simply have held him personally accountable for the actions of the people. The fact of the matter is that Jesus never, in any way, referred to himself as the King of the Jews. He answered Pilate by throwing the question back at him by saying, "You say that I am.", as if to say, "I don't claim to be King of the Jews."

Being King of the Jews wasn't enough to have him crucified. Claiming to be King of the Jews and being rebellious against the Romans was enough to have him crucified. As brutal as the Romans could be they did have a rather rock solid method of justice. They really didn't care much about what the people did among themselves but if they got rebellious against the Romans there was hell to pay. Crucifixion was reserved for those who outwardly and actively rebelled against the Romans, so in order for the Romans to crucify Jesus they must have been convinced that he was rebellious against them. At one point in his interrogation of the Sadducees and Pharisees they asked if it was right to pay taxes to Caesar. If had said no he would have been rebellious. If he had said yes he would have put himself at odds with the authorities who resented paying taxes. He got himself out of that jam by saying, "Render unto Caesar what is Caesars and unto God what is Gods."

Jesus was born and grew up in rather precarious times. He was acutely aware that his message would upset the religious authorities of his day. He was also acutely aware that his message would sooner or later be taken as a being rebellious against Rome. His bottom line was that the only authority that matters is God, and beyond that all that mattered was how people treated each other. He saw through the doctrines and dogmas to the tyranny the religious authorities held over people's lives, while at the same time keeping the ordinary people under control and making them-selves fat and wealthy at the expense of the ordinary people. The tyranny of taxes wasn't only coming from Rome; it was coming from the taxes people had to pay to the Temple hierarchy. You remember the story of the money changers; how they cheated people out of what little money they had by demanding that they exchange their money for the Temple money at about something like ten cents on the dollar. Like I said, to Jesus God is the only authority that matters and beyond that all that matters is how people treat each other because the authority of God comes from God's love and grace which God hopes and intends we will extend to each other.

Jesus wasn't playing games with politics or doctrines and dogmatics, but he knew full well that sooner or later what he had to say would clash with both the political and doctrinal arenas, and they did. He also knew that if the politics and doctrinal abuse didn't change the whole thing would come crashing down on them, and in 70 AD it did come crashing down. The Jews had become more and more rebellious and the Romans finally stepped in and absolutely destroyed Jerusalem and most all of its inhabitants, banishing them from living in their own homeland or in their own cities. The Jews would have no homeland or a Jerusalem until May 14, 1948 AD. The Jews survived, barely, in various enclaves around Europe and Africa and, as we all know too well, they suffered terrible persecutions along the way. Even today their existence as a people and as a nation is very precarious.

So the point of this rambling tirade is how did anything or anyone survive the Roman destruction of Jerusalem and the Jewish nation? It wasn't safe to be a Jew, but it was relatively safe to be a Christian; not that the early Christians had it easy with the Romans either; they suffered their persecutions too. All the early Christians were Jews and to them Jesus was their Messiah, so, over a long period of time the Jewish-now-Christians morphed their faith into something not Jewish. Also, the early Church welcomed non-Jews; Gentiles in their midst. Where the Jews had been very exclusive, these new Christians were very inclusive. Gradually they gave up Hebrew as their native language and adopted Greek, the common language of the Roman Empire. Though their Christian faith had very much been founded on Judaism, they were no longer Jews and that set the stage for the Roman Emperor, Constantine to legalize Christianity in 311 AD and for the eventual adoption as the Christian faith as the official faith of the Roman Empire in 380 AD. Those were some long and painful centuries and the Christian Church that emerged was radically different than what Jesus had envisioned as a community of faith and the early Church took form in. Essentially the Church took over the form of the Roman government. The Emperor became the Pope. The Roman Senate became the College of Cardinals. The regional governors like Herod and Pilate became Bishops, and the local governors became Priests.

It's important to note that the Gospels were not written down, formally, until after the destruction of Jerusalem, actually as an attempt to save the Gospel stories after the destruction of Jerusalem.

They probably were carried on primarily by oral tradition for quite some time and the few very early manuscripts we have are incomplete. Again, reading and writing were confined to a very select few. Mark is the earliest Gospel probably written just before or just after the fall of Jerusalem. Matthew, Mark and Luke all had a common form of the Gospel that they based their stories on which we call the Q document because scraps of it were forum in the caves of Qumran. John comes out of a totally different tradition altogether. As to who actually wrote the Gospels is an open question. It doubtful that the four presumed Gospel writers wrote them themselves; it's unlikely they could read or write, but it is quite possible that whoever did write them down heard the stories originally from those in whose names they were written.

What did happen in the process of writing them down and in all the editing they went through over the years was that the original Jewish flavor and intent was Romanized, and this was done, in part, to make Christianity more palatable to the Roman population, and it also reflects how the Roman population interpreted Christianity according to their own world view. What we end up with is a Romanized version of the person and the ministry of Jesus Christ. There are aspects of the Gospel stories that are actually incompatible with Jewish traditions and beliefs. Jews would not entertain the notion that God could or would become a human being: be fully God and fully man; be God incarnate. The Romans believed that their Emperor was God incarnate. Jews would not entertain the notion that virgin birth was either possible or necessary. Many of the Roman emperors claimed to have come into being in a virgin birth. Whether or not Jesus was fully human or fully God has been and is one of the most divisive issues the Church has ever faced. And, to me, it's not a necessary question: it's a question we really don't to answer and either answer is misleading to the heart and soul of Jesus' message and ministry.

I don't challenge the historical accuracy of the Gospel accounts to try to disillusion anyone, or pop someone's bubble or to challenge the truth of what Christ's life and ministry were and are all about. I totally respect and even cherish all the Bible stories because I recognize the power of the reality of myth. The meaning of the stories is not dependent on whether or not they are historically accurate. All myths originate in some form of a real event or experience. The myths of the Bible originate in the all powerful and all encompassing love and grace of God. Like I said at the beginning, the bottom line for Jesus was and is that the only authority that matters is God, and beyond that all that matters was how people treat each other. That's the Gospel in a nutshell. Doctrine and Dogma, rituals and traditions don't embody or empower that love and grace, and the only practices that really matter is how we treat other people.

In the end, and in the beginning, God is ultimately a mystery and I take great comfort in that truth. We build doctrines and dogmas, rituals and traditions and stories of all shapes and sizes to try to flesh out the mystery that God is. That doesn't in any way mean that our doctrines, dogmas, rituals, traditions and stories are wrong or bogus, but we have to remember to keep ourselves open to the mystery that is behind them; to hear the stories behind the stories, to hear the truth behind the truth, to know the love and grace that is poured out on us and all creation and know we are loved beyond measure and are called to do the same for each other.

Prayers

Our God help us find comfort in knowing that you are God and we're not. Help us let you be the mystery that you are knowing that you are indeed a loving and gracious mystery. Help us read the scriptures knowing that they are not the last word cast in stone forever and ever, but they are doors that open onto and into your mystery and can lead us ever deeper into the personal and communal faith we share. Help us know and find delight in the truth that you are indeed still speaking. You didn't close the door on the power of your presence when the ink dried. You can be and are as real to us as those who lived out the Bible stories and those who wrote them down.

Help us remember that the words of our mouths and the meditations of our hearts are our own, not yours. Help the words of our mouths and the meditations of our hearts be vehicles through which we and others can hear your still, small voice speaking to us right here and now in the midst of the worlds we live in. Amen.

The Door Is Open

When I was back in seminary our Pastoral Care professor told us that when the Church opens the door to the world we had better be prepared for whoever or whatever might come in. He also told us that any Church that does not open its doors wide to the whole world is not doing or being what a church should be. As we approach the fiftieth anniversary of the Poor People's March on Washington, I am reminded of many times, places and situations in which I have seen the Church close its doors on the world, but also many times, places and situations in which the Church has kept its doors wide open and welcomed the world in with its arms wide open.

When I was growing up I had the best of both worlds. We lived in then-rural East Farmington, but my folks had a cutlery store in downtown Hartford, so I was exposed the ethnicity of the inner city and I was comfortable with it. My mother typed theses and books for Hartford Seminary students and faculty so there was a steady stream of people from all over the world in and out of our home. In retrospect my parents; more so my father talked the talk of racism, but I never saw them walk the walk of racism. In fact, when riots consumed the North End of Hartford after Martin Luther King was assassinated, my parents gave the North End barbers who had lost their businesses free credit for barber tools so they could get started again.

At the same time, I grew up in a very white Church in a very white town, which, at the time, seemed quite intent on keeping it that way. Though today the Farmington Church takes great pride, and rightly so, in their role in freeing, housing and educating the former slaves who took over the slave ship Amistad and claimed their freedom, I was well grown up before that story went public. I was in grammar school when the bussing program started that brought Black, inner city kids out to the suburbs. My Senior Minister, Harland Lewis, was a very progressive man who took the Gospel call to openness and inclusion very seriously and he put forth the notion that maybe our Church should invite some of the Black people from the Horace Bushnell Church in the North End out to one of our services. That notion was not well received. My father was the Senior Deacon at the time and though I don't remember the details I do remember often and long meetings between my father and Mr. Lewis, when I was told to stay in my room and do my homework. The Church finally agreed to invite some of the Black choir members from Horace Bushnell to join our choir for a concert, which was not well attended. One Sunday some of the Horace Bushnell choir members came to the regular Sunday service. All I really remember about that is that it only happened once. The bussing program soon came to an end and so did our relations with Horace Bushnell. Bringing "them" out to "our" space was not a good idea. That's not really opening our doors to the world. The doors were locked unless we invited "them" in. The goal of our society and culture is not that all people will become wealthy, white suburbanites. The goal of our society is that all people will be respected for who they are, and the doors will be open between our differences.

I was twelve when the Poor People's March on Washington was planned and held and Mr. Lewis told the diaconate that he wanted to attend and participate. That notion was not well received either. My father was still the Senior Deacon and I remember more often and long meetings between my father and Mr. Lewis. The second time around I was a little more curious and bold and I asked to know what was going on. They told me that some people didn't want Mr. Lewis to go to the Poor People's March. I essentially asked "Why not?", and for the first time that I can remember the reality of racism was verbalized in my home. Ended up that Mr. Lewis went to Washington, my father had defended his right to do so, some people actually left the Church over the whole issue; some because they were racists and intended to stay that way; some because they wanted no part of a Church that would challenge Mr. Lewis' right to go or allow him to speak out against racism. Troubled times, but we've come a long way. The Church was packed when Mr. Lewis came back from Washington and he was free to talk about the March and what it all meant and he was very well received.

About that same time, soon after the March on Washington, I went with my mother on a Senior Pilgrim Fellowship field trip down to North Carolina. She was a chaperone and invited me to come along for the experience, and what an experience it was. We spent the first night in a Hispanic Church in Philadelphia. Again, I was familiar and comfortable with people of other ethnicities, but it was quite an experience to be totally immersed in a different ethnic community. The second day and night we spent in Washington DC and I saw all the magnificent buildings and statues and the places that were packed to over flowing during the March. The next day we went down to North Carolina. We stopped for lunch at a rest stop in southern Virginia and for the for the first time I saw all the "Whites Only" signs on the restrooms, drinking fountains and restaurants. There weren't any Blacks around because they obviously weren't welcome.

We ended up at an orphanage associated with Elon College, in the town of Elon College, North Carolina, where my mother had attended and graduated from years before. The Pilgrim Fellowship kids went and worked at the orphanage. My mother took me on tours of the college, the area and to track down some of her old friends. Some of her old friends took us out to dinner one evening, to a "Whites Only" restaurant, and I remember when anything came up in the conversation about race they were blatantly racist and the "N" word was common language. After it was all done I expressed my displeasure to my mother and she told me that that's the way some people are and they're the kind of people who are going to have to be changed if we ever might be freed from our own slavery to our own racism: powerful, motherly words.

In 1969 I packed my bags, put on my best tie-dyed pants, shirt and jacket, brushed my long hair back over my ears and took a plane ride to Elon College, North Carolina. I was not well received and would have just as soon hopped back on the next plane heading north, but I decided to give it a try. I did my best to ignore the cat calls of "Hey, look, there's a hip-eye." but it hurt. After a while I found fellowship with a bunch of other "hip-eyes". It had been just the year before that Elon College had accepted their first black student, Elmer, and then only on a day student basis. Elmer joined our "hip-eye" group and we soon became good friends. There was a common bond in being hated because you were black or being hated because you were a "Hip-eye". We went on a trip to North Carolina A&M College where Elmer wanted to introduce us to some of his friends. We had a great time together, and they showed us where race riots had taken place a couple years earlier and the college had made no attempt to repair the bullet holes in the walls and windows. The following year, Elon admitted its first fulltime, live in black students; two of them and assigned one of them, John, with me as roommates. Some of the white students, even some "hip-eyes" were appalled and wanted me to go to the Dean and get them roomed together. I asked John if he wanted to make that happen and he said "No, if we're going to really get integrated this is how it starts." I totally agreed. I dropped out of Elon at the end of that semester when they closed my beloved theater group, which was all that kept me at Elon in the first place, and as I signed out with the Dean I said I hoped nobody thought this had anything to do with my black roommate. He groveled in apology for letting that happen; I walked out the door, slamming it behind me, and never looked back.

I learned a whole lot about racism during the years I worked in the North End of Hartford with Habitat for Humanity; mainly how complex, confounded and confusing the whole issue is. Racism is anything BUT a black and white issue, if you'll excuse the pun. It is a whole mixed bag of cultural, traditional and ethnic issues. I confess I used to lump all black people together and all Hispanic people together and all white people together as separate entities. The truth is anything but that. Within the Black community are multiple sub-communities from American Blacks; descendents of slavery; groups of any number of Caribbean islands and South American countries; all Blacks outside of Africa are, in one way or another descendents of slavery; true Africans from any number of countries, and to some extent they each maintain their own ethnic communities but in many ways they are all blended together, and believe you me, they don't all get along together. The biggest divide is between the white community in general and the Black/Hispanic community in general. That's where we still have lots of work to do: opening those doors.

Racism is a door that must be opened. The door can be opened or closed from either side. Racism can become a prison that locks you in yourself and out of other's lives. One doesn't just inflict racism on others; one inflicts racism on oneself. Racism is indeed a two edged sword which cuts both ways and we all would benefit from tearing down those walls and opening those doors. It never has been an easy challenge; we've come a long ways, but we've got a long ways to go, and I'm not just talking about whites getting rid of their racism; I'm talking about all sides burying the hatchet and letting their ways be changed.

The UCC has a relatively new slogan that goes like this: "Whoever you are . . . Wherever you are in life's journey . . . You are Welcome here."

That, to me, is the sound of an opening door; an open door. The Church not only must just be an open door; the Church must show the world what a truly open door looks and acts like. Christ came to open the door so God's love and grace can not only come in, but that it can go out into the whole world. That is what we: the people of the Church are called to do and be. We open our doors not only to let God's love and grace in, but to let it out; to make it real and alive in real people's lives: all people of all ages, genders, races, tongues and colors.

So let's open the doors of our hearts, minds and spirits and let the love and grace of God come in and then carry it out through the doors of our lives into our worlds. The door is open.

Prayers

Our God, Lord of life, love and grace help us open the doors of our hearts, minds and spirits and not only just let you in, but let you out into our world through our words and deeds. Help us realize that being shut up in the locked rooms of racism, sexism, prejudice and paranoia do us as much harm as they do anyone else. Help us see beyond colors, hear beyond languages, understand beyond cultural, traditional and ethnic differences and come to know and appreciate all others as being your beloved children.

There is so much animosity, unnecessary distrust and unwarranted fear festering out there, if not within us, that needs to be healed by the reality of your love and grace. Help that love and grace find their way in our doors and out our doors and windows that we may truly be the Church you call and enable us to be.

Life is not easy sometimes, Lord: we have our physical, emotional, mental and spiritual issues that weigh us down. Help us heal, God, help us heal. Life is also full of big and little blessings. Help us count them and cherish them and give thanks for them. Amen.

Glory and Honor

God must think an awful lot of us to crown us with glory and honor. God must have some great expectations for us human beings. God must love us a lot. God gives us dominion over all God's critters, a notion that we, unfortunately, have often abused. Having dominion over something does not mean that "we" are somehow better than "them" or that we can destroy "them" at whim: "them" being all other living things and the ecosystem that gives and sustains life itself. The population of the United States has more than tripled in the last century, from about one million to about 3 million. The population of the world has also more than tripled in the last century, from about 2 billion to more than six billion and the growth is accelerating. Even with the vast numbers of people who die of old age, or anything but old age: from famine to war, the population is still growing and the growth is accelerating. The problem is not that the earth and its ecosystem are not capable of sustaining all the people on the planet. The problem is how we distribute the fruits of our planet and ecosystem. I think a better word to describe what God expects of us is not to have dominion over our part of God's Creation, but that we would be good stewards of God's Creation and make sure everybody has what they need.

We have come to the point in the evolution of our population where we are consuming what is available faster than it can be renewed. And so often much so much of what we harvest from Creation is wasted. Countless numbers of sharks are killed only for their fins. Vast numbers of elephants are killed only for their ivory. Vast numbers of rhinoceros are killed only for their horns. Millions of tons of corn are harvested not for food but for ethanol. The factory boat fishing industry kills and throws away seafood sometimes more than they keep. We have come to the point in the evolution of our population where we are consuming what is available faster than it can be renewed, and still thousands of people starve to death daily. We have to reconsider what it means to be good stewards of God's Creation, ourselves included.

Time was when we could just dump all our garbage into the rivers and/or the oceans and it would just wash away. Then the neighbors down the river started complaining and soon the rivers were polluted to the point of dying and not being able to sustain life. I worked in Seymour, CT in the summer of 1971, downstream from the Goodyear sneaker factory. The entire Naugatuck valley reeked of hot rubber and the color of the river would change according to what color of sneaker they were making at the time. It was kind of a joke that the Naugatuck River was lined with rubber. The truth is that it was. There hadn't been a fish in the lower Naugatuck River for years at that time. The Good News is that the Naugatuck River has been reclaimed and cleaned up and fish abound and you can actually eat them, unlike the fish in the lower Housatonic River which are contaminated with the invisible carcinogen of PCBs.

Time was when we could assure ourselves that there would always be plenty of fish in the sea, birds in the air and animals in the wilderness, clean water to drink and clean air to breathe. We can't make that assumption anymore and we are called by God, our Creator, to be good stewards; the only ones who can and must stop the destruction and enable the healing to begin and continue. Great strides have been taken and great accomplishments and successes have happened and are happening, but our responsibility to be good stewards increases proportionately to the increases in overall population. Our population growth is like a really big ocean liner. If we find we have to change course it can take a lot of time and distance to make the move; more time and distance than the Titanic had. But it's a beautiful Summer morning here in Stafford Springs, my new home town, and the point of all of this is that we have to take responsibility to keep it that way. The Good News is that God says we can do it. The hard part is believing that we can do it, and God is there to help with that too.

It will be a very complicated process to change the course of the effects of our population growth. It's not just pollution and damage to the ecosystem; change is needed in how we value Creation. When I lived in Bangor, Maine, I would occasionally drive across the state and I had to go through the town of Rumford which was built around a massive paper mill. If there was an inversion in the atmosphere or the air was very still the stench was totally unbearable and one's eyes burned by the time you got through town. Once I had to stop and get gas and I asked the attendant how he could stand living there. He said first that you get used to it, and then he added that the smell was the smell of the hundreds of jobs that kept Rumford going. The good news is that they were able to clean up the paper mill emissions and still keep their jobs. Slowly but surely we are beginning to recognize the value of, and even the profit from, going green: being aware of the need to preserve what we have and even enhance what we have by using renewable resources.

God must think an awful lot of us to crown us with glory and honor. God must have some great expectations for us human beings. God must love us a lot. God gives us minds with which to invent all sorts of wonderful things. Along the way we have made some mistakes and have done some damage, but we do have the ability to fix our mistakes and repair our damage. The earth will always repair itself if we stop doing damage, step back and allow it to do so. God gives us hearts with which to have compassion, even love for one another. We have to combine the two and overcome the greed, indifference and apathy that make room for the injustices of some having so much while others have little or nothing; while some live upriver where the river is still clean, while others suffer from our waste and pollution downstream.

It can be very, very difficult to wrap our heads around the magnitude of the problems we face with pollution, waste and population growth, and God's crowning us with glory and honor is a big boost to our self esteem and our faith that God has faith in us and our ability to solve our problems. This is Good News. As much as we may find ourselves confounded by the problems that surround us and find their ways from within us, God has never and never will give up on us. We are crowned with glory and honor; we are God's beloved children.

The change can start on any given Sunday morning, or any other morning, afternoon or evening of any day when we can kick back, relax and enjoy a few moments of peace and tranquility like we have here. Creation, for the most part, is very peaceful, placid and plentiful. The abundance of God's love is obvious in the plenty of Creation. Yes, there are times when it would seem that Creation is our worst enemy; when earthquakes shatter towns, homes and lives; when tsunamis wash away everything we have taken for granted; when senseless and meaningless death takes our loved ones from us; but we are an integral part of God's Creation: we experience the reality of life and death, growth and change at every twist and turn in life, just as do all the other creatures in God's wondrous Creation. God never has nor never will give up on us. We must never give up on God.

From day one of the human condition we have postured ourselves somewhere between the need to affirm who and what we are and what changes we are faced with and need to go through in order to survive; we have had to adapt, change, make something new, allow something new to happen, make something new happen, and allow ourselves to let go of that which once worked and now no longer does work.

Our world abounds with things that no longer work: racism no longer works, sexism no longer works, homophobia no longer works; the great divide between the have-too-much-of and those-who-have-nothing no longer works; pollution, waste and indifference no longer work; war and rumors of war no longer work. We cannot go back to the twentieth, the nineteenth, the eighteenth, or, God help us, long before that to claim that once upon a time, long ago and far away, we had it all right and that's the way it should always be.

The sun comes every morning and each day is a brand new day filled with some of the same-old-same-old, but always ushering in something new. Something new; "Behold I am making all things new." To desperately hang on to the past is to deny the future of all that God intends, promises and assures us of. The past and the present, for the most part, are not anything to be necessarily proud of or ashamed of, but are stepping stones in the rivers of life that can lead us from one shore to another; to something new, something wondrous; something that shapes and reflects our crowns of glory and honor.

Here we have a wonderful opportunity to engage the simple beauties of God's Creation. So let all this sink in deeply. It's not just the peaceful setting. It's the people we are and the people we are with. The history we all share, both short term and long term. The families and friendships we have or are making. The lives we share, have shared, and look forward to.

We are all beloved children of God; we are all crowned in glory and honor. That is the really Good News in the face of all the bad news our world can confront us with.

Prayers

Our God, for all the wonders, beauties and mysteries of this wonderful Creation that we are a part of we stand in awe and thank you with everything we are. You enable us to affect this wonderful Creation; in some ways we do have dominion over it, but in more ways we are called by you to be good stewards of what you have given us. You give us the ability to interact with Creation our own creative ways, but with that ability comes a great responsibility; a responsibility to use what you have given us wisely, equally and lovingly, respecting, having compassion for, even loving the people and all the living things we share this Creation with.

There was a time when we believed that wherever there was plenty there would always be more than enough but we are faced with the reality that that may not be as true as we once thought. Countless creatures have gone extinct over the millions of years that life has been on this planet, most because they could not adapt to the changes that evolved over the eons, but we have caused the extinction of many species not out of natural changes, but out of waste and greed. Help us be mindful that in truth all creatures have the same right to safety and life as we do. The plants and animals we depend on for food can do reproduce and are renewable, but help us not push the limits to how renewable they are, or we are.

O God, there are so many people who suffer so needlessly from not having the basic necessities that come with simply being alive and so many do not survive. Help us be mindful that when some have so much they bear the responsibility of sharing with those in need. Amen.

Little Children

When a child is born they are a blank slate. I'm sure that there are many genetic dispositions that will kick in as the child develops, but right at birth, if not even before birth, the child is learning and growing; the child is becoming the person they will eventually be. Genetics don't determine what language the child will learn to speak, read and write. They don't teach a child how to tie their shoes. Everything that child will ever know, ever understand and ever do will be taught to that child by someone else. The vast, vast, vast majority of children are born to parents who unconditionally love them and devote their whole beings: hearts, souls, bodies and minds to loving them, taking care of them and teaching them what it will be and what it is to be the person they will become. I like to say that a child is born expecting only one thing: to be loved. Expecting is too strong a word. A newborn doesn't expect anything, but the one essential thing they need is unconditional and wholistic love and the people around them are the only ones who can love them. Newborn love is wholistic: it is physical, it is mental; it is emotional; it is spiritual all at once. When a child is born they are a blank slate and it is up to those around that child; those who love that child to fill in the blanks.

When my first daughter was born the first thing she did was open her eyes and stare into mine; deep into mine; not just looking at me but looking into me and I was looking into her. I was the first person she saw. It was the same with my other two daughters, but I guess I was expecting it to happen by then. The eyes; the looking into my soul by my first daughter blew my mind, or maybe it's better to say she blew into my mind and I into hers.

Eye contact is a truly miraculous occurrence. What is the first thing we do when we meet someone? We look into each other's eyes. Even when just passing strangers on the street or even when we're driving we make eye contact with each other; most of the time anyhow. I stop at a stop sign and I wonder if that person, or one of four persons, is going to follow protocol or pull out in front of me. They are wondering the same thing about me. So what we do? We make eye contact even through our windshields across the intersection. If a person doesn't make eye contact I am leery of them, and the odds are pretty good that they are not going to follow protocol.

The same is true with the vast majority of animals. Stop at a stop sign and a dog is there in the car next to you with its head hanging out the window and what's the first thing it does? It makes eye contact. Drive by a house and there's a cat sitting in a window. What's the first thing it does? They make eye contact; even through the window, across the road and you're driving by in a car. Go to a zoo and all of the animals make eye contact with you and each other, most of the time. Sometimes they are so bored or miserable that they don't want to make eye contact. Not making eye contact when interacting with another person or an animal is not normal; and it is a sign that something could be wrong. As a pastor and as a semi-professional counselor I make careful note of the nature of the eye contact with the person I am with. Not making eye contact is a sure sign that everything's not right with that person. I once was introduced to a wolf that was as tame as a wild animal could be, but we were warned not to make steady eye contact with it. A passing glance was OK but a continuous stare was threatening to the wolf, especially as it was in a new situation with strangers and its handler couldn't guarantee how long it would stay tame.

I'm sure this phenomenon has puzzled people ever since they came to be able to ask why to something. It's so normal and natural that we just sort of take it for granted. Something happens between us; to both or all of us when we make eye contact. The aborigines of Australia and a few other indigenous groups around the world take eye contact to a new level; at least new to us. It is very common that two or more will gather in a group and make eye contact for a while and then go as a pair or a group to do something together. No words were said, but obviously something was communicated. That is true for many forms of animals. There is limited vocal communication but obviously communication happens through eye contact, and sometimes even without eye contact. Mental telepathy . . . ? How else can one explain how old friends and long time lovers know what each other is doing and what they are going to do or say next without saying a word and even being miles if not years apart?

A long standing science experiment takes two good friends or lovers and puts them in separate rooms, one with a deck of playing cards. One takes a card and concentrates on it and the other, in the other room, tries to visualize the card the other person is looking at. It is more than common that the person trying to visualize the others card will get it right well above 50 percent, when common mathematical odds suggest a much lower rate of success. Put the two people where they can make eye contact and the rates go even higher. A recent scientific experiment attached brain wave probes to two people's heads and asked one to think of a certain event or thing. They measured the brain patterns in the sender and when they made eye contact the same patterns emerged in the receiver's brains and the longer they stared at each other the more their brain patterns became the same.

So here I am on page 3 of this tirade and you're probably wondering what the heck all of this has to do with little children. I am trying to remind us how little children learn because how and what they learn shapes the rest of their lives. Children are sponges absorbing everything around them for the first time and taking it all in and if they are fortunate to have unconditionally loving parents and teachers they will learn to unconditionally love. They believe what we are teaching them without question because they can unconditionally trust these parents and teachers.

Unfortunately, sooner or later, most every person encounters a situation in which this trust is somehow broken. In a good situation a person learns to just be leery; to know there are some people you can't trust but there are lots of others you can trust. In a worst case scenario a person comes to not trust anybody. The younger a person is when this trust is broken the more likely it is that they will come to not trust anybody and then street gangs and drugs and violence and sociopathic behavior sets in.

Jesus is acknowledging that there are lots of people one can't trust, for a multitude of reasons, but one can always trust God and Jesus is inviting us to open ourselves up to God like little children open themselves up to their brand new world. The essential question here is how one comes to know God and so one can truly open oneself up to God. This is the root source of where my tirades about doctrine and dogma come from. We cannot learn about God only through doctrines and dogmas. We cannot encounter God only through our knowledge and logic; our ologies. We cannot experience God only through our traditions, though our traditions can truly be reminders of previous encounters with God. Our encounter with God must be as open and wholistic as the way a child encounters their brand new world. We can learn about God in a variety of ways, but to truly encounter God we have to look God in the eyes; we have to see and hear and feel and know the reality of God as God is, even if God is years and miles away, which God isn't. We have to open our minds to the mind of God. God is as present as the air we breathe; as wholistic as our lives are.

The way we can best truly encounter God is holistically, which includes the dimension of spirituality, which is not by any means a new or different dimension of life, but is inclusive of all the aspects of our perceptions of life all at the same time. In my opinion we, especially the scientific world, have gone way overboard in separating our beings into various categories: our physical beings, our emotional beings, our mental beings, our spiritual beings. It's time to put us back together again, and though all the king's horses and all the king's men can't do it, God can. That is the way we come into this world and that's the way we can come to truly enjoy the miracle that life is.

Jesus is not just inviting us to become as little children; Jesus is telling and assuring us that when it comes to God, we indeed can be children, and not by literally becoming children again. We all have our child living within us. We all can remember the times when we were innocent and curious and wide open to the wonders of life. Maybe that's a hurtful memory, but the Good News is that those good memories are as real as the life we are living right now. That reality is still available to us; it's ours for the asking; it's ours for the opening; it's ours for the reclaiming. It's called faith in something much more present, profound and real than any doctrine or dogma; any ology. It's the holistic encounter with God that we have every time we take a deep breath; every time we open our eyes and look into someone else's eyes; every time we think a thought that we know someone else is thinking; every time we look out on, experience, celebrate and enjoy the miracle that is Creation.

Our encounter with God can be as obvious, direct, real and existential as this moment in the ever present, ever moving continuum we call time; we call life. Do not ever be afraid to open yourselves to God. Open yourselves to God as little children open themselves to life. We can do it. Jesus says so. God says so.

Prayers

Our living, loving God take us back to that time when everything was brand new and wondrous. Rekindle in us our childhood wonder and curiosity and help us focus in on you. Help us see you in our eyes and the eyes of others. Help us hear you in the sounds of Creation, the sounds of music, the sounds of others voices. Help us feel you within us, among us and all around us. Help us sense you with all our senses because you come to us in every way imaginable; not just in our thinking, our logic and our ologies, but in the whole of creation; the whole of our lives.

We know that our relationship with you is awakened in and through our relationships with others: others teach us about you; others show us the ways in which they know you; we get a hint of you, a glimpse of you and then it's up to us to set out to find you, know you and open ourselves to you. We can only do that as children who open ourselves totally to you in total trust and faith.

We know and you know the times in our lives when our trust has been shaken or broken. They are hurtful times, but you tell us and assure us that we can always trust you. You are the light in the darkness, the hope in despair, the life even in death. Empower and enable us to become as little children again and delight in your unconditional love. Amen.

A Big Heart Open to God

Last week "America" magazine: a Jesuit magazine associated with the "National Catholic Review" published a lengthy interview with Pope Francis entitled "A Big Heart Open to God." It is causing quite a stir throughout the Church; within both the Catholic and Protestant Churches. Some Catholics are very threatened and offended by it. Some Catholics applaud it, and the responses I have heard from the Protestant world range from indifference to cynicism to likening it to a much needed and welcomed breath of fresh air. I am of the latter. This is some of the best news I have ever heard coming out of the life of the Church as a whole.

I have always viewed the Catholic Church as being a bastion of ancient and totally inflexible doctrines and dogmas which is in no way my making a judgment. It was simply the truth. Doctrines are the rules of the game and the attitude has always seemed to be that if you don't follow these rules to the letter and play the game of life by these rules then you were out of the game altogether. Dogma is the game itself: a collection of prescribed and proscribed liturgies and rituals that, again, had to be followed and played out to the letter or you would be thrown out of the game. That inflexibility always turned me off to the Catholic Church. That and the incredibly complex and all powerful hierarchy that seemed stuck in the Middle, if not Dark Ages. To me the Catholic Church was the ultimate "We've always done it this way." institution and I could never resolve that inflexibility with the always flexible love and grace of God.

What Pope Francis is saying in his interview is that the love and grace of God are more important than any doctrine or dogma. The person is more important than simply following some rules and any doctrine or dogma that interferes with this personal relation with God is not a good doctrine or dogma. I can hear the walls of the Vatican cracking.

When asked about specific issues like homosexuality, divorce and abortion he doesn't answer the question in some formal doctrinal or dogmatic way. He responds by asking the question "What do you think God thinks of a person who has sinned? What do think God thinks of a person who is homosexual, or has had an abortion, or has been divorced?" He answers his own question by stating, quite simply and profoundly, "God still loves them and cares deeply for them. That is what we, the Church, should be doing also. Let's get away from all this condemnation by doctrine and dogma and get back to be doing what we're supposed to be doing: taking pastoral care of any and all people in our flock." That is a profound diversion from where the Catholic Church has seemingly always stood.

That really resonates deep inside my soul because, as you have probably noticed, that is the heart and soul of my message. Nothing can compromise the love and grace of God and anything that does is doing something very wrong. That message was stirring inside me even as a boy, a young man. I remember asking my confirmation class associate minister. "If God loves everybody so much, how can God send a person to hell for eternity?" He really didn't have an answer but I think he said something like "That's what we believe because that's what the Bible says." He gave me a doctrinal answer: a cast in stone doctrinal answer.

That issue burned inside me for years, even, if not especially in seminary. There I learned that the Bible does *not* describe a literal hell like Dante does or the Catholic Church asserts in their doctrines. There is only one reference to eternal damnation and that is purportedly used by Jesus purely as a metaphor. It's the story in Matthew when he says that Jesus said that at the Last Judgment God would separate the sheep from the goats; the sheep being the ones who gave him something to drink when he was thirsty, food when he was hungry and took care of him when he was sick. The goats were the ones who didn't and they were sent to the eternal fires prepared for the devil and the demons. Matthew is the only one who mentions this at all and when you read it in the original Greek it is obviously of a different literary style. It's like reading along in a book by Kurt Vonnegut and suddenly coming across a paragraph that is written in Shakespearean poetry. It just doesn't fit. It is not blasphemous or unreasonable to assume that some biblical editors and copiers took some liberties in their work, if only to bolster the doctrinal assertions of the times.

When doctrines, dogmas and institutional hierarchies become so inflexible that they cannot respond to the real needs of the people they get in the way of the personal relationship with God that is so basic and so real. People end up worshipping the doctrines and dogmas mistaking them for God's love and grace. People end up worshipping the institution; the Church, not God. In that way the doctrines, dogmas and institutions of the Church actually get in the way of people coming to have a real, personal relationship with God in which they come to really know the love and grace of God.

I didn't really bust out of that issue until I encountered Matthew Fox and Creation Spirituality in which he makes it very clear that the vast majority of traditional doctrines and dogmas are the creation of the institution of the Church and have no basis in biblical fact. The doctrines of Original Sin and Atonement are prime examples. Traditional doctrine asserts that we come into this world totally in sin, condemned to death and eternal punishment, and the only way to get out of that is to be atoned to God, which literally means being made one with the doctrines and dogmas of the Church. That simply is not true. We come into this world; into this blessed creation as blessed creatures and all God wants to do is keep blessing us so that we can bless each other. That is a totally different world view. What happens due to the doctrine of original sin is that if we are condemned we can condemn others, and if we hold the power of atonement we have ultimate power over other people. Erase that equation and you find quite a different world to live in. Matthew Fox is one of many, myself included, who are trying to erase that equation. What blows me away by this interview with Pope Francis is that it appears that he is headed in the same direction. As he says, if a doctrine or dogma gets in the way of the love and grace of God there's something wrong with it.

Here are few more quotes from his interview:

On making changes he says: "I believe that we always need time to lay the foundations for real change."

On being a Jesuit (the Society of Jesus) he says; "The Society of Jesus is an institution in tension . . . always fundamentally in tension. A Jesuit is a person who is not centered on himself. The Society (of Jesus) also looks to a center outside itself; its center is Christ and (Christ's) Church."

On the hierarchy of the Church he says: "We should not even think . . . that 'thinking with the Church' means only thinking with the hierarchy of the Church."

On the role of the Church in the world he says: "The thing the Church needs most today is the ability to heal wounds and to warm the hearts of the faithful: it needs nearness, proximity. I see the Church as a field hospital after battle."

On homosexuality (and others "sins") he says, as I explained before: "A person once asked me, in a provocative manner, if I approved of homosexuality. I replied with another question: 'tell me: when God looks at a gay person, does (God) endorse the existence of this person with love, or reject and condemn this person?' We must always consider the person (first)"

On dogmatics and doctrine he says: "The dogmatic and moral teachings of the Church are not all equivalent. The Church's pastoral ministry cannot be obsessed with the transmission of a disjointed multitude of doctrines to be imposed insistently."

On Women in the life of the Church he says: "It is necessary to broaden the presence of women in the Church . . . Women are asking deep questions that must be addressed. The Church cannot be herself without the women . . . (Women are) essential to the Church. Mary is more important than (all) the bishops (put together)."

On finding God he says: "Finding God in all things is not an "empirical eureka". When we would like to encounter God, we would like to verify (God) immediately by an empirical method. But you cannot meet God this way. God is found in the gentle breeze perceived by Elijah."

On maintaining meaningless traditions and conservatism he says: "If the Christian is a restorationist, a legalist, if he wants everything clear and safe, then he will find nothing."

On solving practical, existential issues of faith he says: "Ours is not a faith lab, but a journey faith, a historical faith." (Rooted in the reality that is the present)

On other faiths and religions he says. "The view of the Church's teaching as a monolith to defend without nuance or different understandings is wrong."

These are all profound statements reflecting a big heart that is open to God: open to God, not doctrines and dogmas, not hierarchies, not institutions but open to God in a truly spiritual way. This could be a tremendously important development in the life of the Church; the whole Church. Even though our beloved United Church of Christ is as liberal and progressive as it can get, I still occasionally encounter colleagues and friends who insist on playing the game by a strict set of arbitrary rules: doctrines and dogmas; doctrines and dogmas that get in the way of doing and being what the Church should be doing and being: loving all our brothers and sisters as God loves us all. Nothing can separate us from the love of God as we see it, know it and experience it in Christ; in the personal, spiritual relationship Christ offers us. If something is separating us from the love of God we have to take a stand, as Martin Luther did and Pope Francis has done: to proclaim the truth that we are all indeed set free by the love and grace of God and nothing should get in the way of that freedom.

Prayers

Our God help us take off our blinders, open our doors and windows wide; open our hearts and minds and spirits to the wondrous mystery that you are: a living loving mystery that is as close and real as the air we breathe.

Contrary to what has been taught for so long by so many, you don't nor will you ever condemn us. Your love creates us, sustains us and is available to us at every twist and turn in life. We can put on our blinders, close and lock our doors; we can hide from you but you will never hide from us.

We thank you for the wonderful gift that is our minds. We are curious. We want to understand things. We want to figure things out and explain them in a clear and concise way and to some extent we can figure you out, understand you and explain you, but the truth is you are always a mystery that is beyond our full comprehension. All we can know about you is what you have revealed to us and what you have revealed to us is the wondrous breadth and depth of your love for us and all of your Creation made known most personally in Christ. Help us be Christ's to each other as you are Christ to us all. Amen.

On Being Made Whole

We live in a breaking and broken world and in a breaking and broken society. We live with a breaking and broken government and with a breaking and broken economy. We live in and with a fractured Church amidst many other fractured religions; fractured into factions that at best tolerate each other and at worst do everything they can to destroy each other. It t'ain't a pretty picture and there are no rose colored glasses or Pollyannaish perspectives that can make that bad news go away. So where is the good news? We are broken and what can make us whole again?

We assume that we live in a democracy and at the heart of a democracy is the assumption that we all must respect the will of the majority and deeper into the heart of the matter is the assumption that we all must respect each other. Democracies are supposed to work out their differences internally and peacefully, but that t'ain't happening these days. One of the phrases that really freaks me out and honestly scares me is "All the American people . . ." want this or that or some other thing when obviously a small, self interested minority agenda is being attempted to be slammed down the throats of everybody else. Now don't in any way get me wrong here: I am not taking sides here. You can find that strategy being used by any and all sides against any and all other sides. It's the strategy that bothers me. That strategy assumes that if someone makes a claim about something loud and long enough others will come to believe it whether its' true or not. If people believe a claim that "All the American people . . ." want something then people are apt to say something like, "Well, if everybody else wants that, then so should I." That is not how a democracy works. We are not all like sheep just following a mob or hive mentality.

At the heart of the matter for me is the question of what are the ground rules in all of this? What is the focal point? What is the ethical foundation on which these actions are based? One of my favorite classes in seminary was "Ethics", Christian Ethics in particular but also in comparison to other ethical systems, in which I learned that ethics are not about WHAT is right or wrong but WHY some things are right and some things are wrong. Ethics are the reasons why some things are deemed good and others are not. I think the reason that we are in the midst of such confusion, chaos and conflict is that we, as a society, a nation and even as a culture do not have a common ethical foundation and without a common ethical foundation we indeed are like sheep gone astray. What some think is right others think is wrong and we have no common ground to negotiate from. Neither side cares what the other side thinks about what is right or wrong and what one side does in the name of right has no respect for what the other side thinks is wrong and back and forth like a ping pong game.

I believe we once did have a common ethical foundation or at least much more of one than we do today. I believe that it is true to say that we once shared a common ethical foundation based on Christian and Jewish ethics which are expressed in attitudes like love your neighbor as yourself; respect each other if only because we are all beloved children of God; live according to the ten commandments; take care of the poor. I would be wearing rose colored glasses and thinking like Pollyanna if I pretended that we truly and totally lived by those ground rules in everything we did, but there was a common denominator that certainly influenced our big decisions and major actions. Those ground rules are all but gone.

Where did they go? I think is fair to say that those foundations started cracking when one atheist was able to change the law of the land eliminating any and all references to God by or in any public place: no prayer, preaching or worship in schools, no religious symbols or rituals in public places or government places. We kicked God out of the schools so unless the children go to a church, synagogue or mosque they will have no exposure to God and God's ethics. So now we are in the midst of the third generation of people in which the majority has had no experience of God whatsoever. So why should they care about anything being right or wrong? So even though we still have chaplains opening sessions for the various branches and forms of government with prayer; we still print on our money "In God we trust." and according to the pledge of allegiance we still believe we are "One nation under God" there no guts to those statements; there is no meaning in those statements because there is meaning only in those statements if the ethics that should come along with them are there, and they're not.

The only thing than can bring us together as a people is a shared common denominator. Most of us Christians assume at the base of our ethical response to our faith in God that one way or another we have a responsibility to care about and take care of each other; to not act in our own self interests at the expense of others; to care about and take care of the poor; to spread the wealth evenly; to not try to slam our faith beliefs down other's throats at their expense. The base of our ethical beliefs is that we are to love our neighbor as ourselves and, above all else, not hurt anybody else; to not be greedy and indifferent. Without that ethical foundation or one similar to it people can and do say quite openly and bluntly, "Why not? Why should I care about my neighbors let alone love them? Why shouldn't I hurt them?" if not in so many words then most certainly in their actions. How else can you explain why CEOs could get millions of dollars in bonuses when they are being fired for squandering other people's money and making them lose their homes? How else can you explain how Congress can shut down the government putting hundreds thousands of people out of work and denying essential services to the poor and the sick and do their best to derail the Affordable Care Act when they don't cut their own salaries and they have the most complete insurance coverage in the nation?

That kind of brokenness I don't know how to heal and make whole. I wish I had or there was a simple answer to that whole mess. The only solution I can conceive of would be to find someone or some group that could call them into account and make them see that they are broken and they have to change their ways in order to be made whole and healed so that our nation and our world could be made whole and healed. I believe the Church is a group that could do just that and many denominations, including our UCC, are doing just that, or at least doing their best trying.

What I do know is where healing and wholeness can come from and do come from. They come from the love and grace of God. God creates us as whole, healthy people. We break ourselves and each other. God is always right there ready to help us heal and be made whole again. We have to open ourselves to God for that to happen.

Communion is a ritual, a symbol of that which makes us one; that which makes us whole. It is a symbol of the ethical foundation of our faith: we are called to love as we are loved by God. It is a symbol of that which can heal us and make us whole as persons because the only way a person can be healed and made whole is by being a part of a community that is healthy and whole and that is what the Church is called to be. Sometimes we get it right, sometimes we get it wrong, but we are on the ongoing path to being healthy and whole in the love and grace of God.

As Paul says, "There is neither slave nor free, Jew nor Greek, male or female, (and I would add: there is neither Republican nor Democrat, liberal nor conservative), for we are called to be one by and in the love and grace of God. In God we already are one. In that truth; in that faith we can believe that we can and will be healed and made whole.

Prayers

Our living, loving God we confess the brokenness of ourselves, of our institutions and even the brokenness of our faith. We come to you asking that you help us heal and be made whole in all the ways we are broken.

You create us whole but we tend to fall apart and get broken as we go through life. Sometimes we get it right, sometimes we get it wrong and sometimes we don't get it at all. Your love and grace assure us that we can be made whole again; we can be made well again.

We ask that you help instill in our institutions, our public servants and our leaders a sense of your ethic of love. You make it available to each and all of us at every twist and turn, but as of late it seems that so many have turned away from you, forsaken you for their own self interests and their own self righteous agendas, some even proclaiming that what they are doing and seeking is all done in your name when obviously it is not.

Make each and all of us the helpers and healers we need so much. Enable us to be able to help ourselves, each others and our wider communities be made whole in your love and grace. Amen.

Edwards Brothers Malloy
Thorofare, NJ USA
May 2, 2014